Opus 80

Verleger und Autor danken dem UAA Ungers Archiv für Architekturwissenschaft, Köln, insbesondere Sophia Ungers, Anja Sieber-Albers und Bernd Grimm, für die Zusammenarbeit bei der Veröffentlichung dieses Buches.

Publisher and author thank the UAA Ungers Archiv für Architekturwissenschaft, Cologne, especially Sophia Ungers, Anja Sieber-Albers und Bernd Grimm, for the cooperation in publishing this book.

UAA Ungers Archiv für Architekturwissenschaft

Oswald Mathias Ungers
Haus Belvederestraße 60
Köln-Müngersdorf

Essay
Wolfgang Pehnt

Photographien / Photographs
Walter Ehmann
Bernd Grimm
Dieter Leistner
Stefan Müller

Edition Axel Menges

Herausgeber/Editor: Axel Menges

ISBN 978-3-930698-80-9

Druck und Bindearbeiten/Printing and binding: Graspo CZ, a.s., Zlín, Tschechische Republik/Czech Republic

Übersetzung ins Englische/Translation into English: Ilze Klavina
Gestaltung/Design: Axel Menges

Inhalt

Contents

Wolfgang Pehnt

Haus Belvederestraße 60, Köln-Müngersdorf

Wenn Architekten ein Haus für sich selber bauen, sollte man meinen, sie erfüllten sich einen Berufswunsch. Sie können anwenden, was sie gelernt haben. Kein Bauherr redet ihnen darein, weil sie selbst die Bauherren sind. Sie können die Form und den Grundriß wählen, von denen sie meinen, daß sie den eigenen Vorstellungen, Verhaltensweisen, Wohnbedürfnissen und denen ihrer Familien gemäß sind. Sie können ihren Mitmenschen zu verstehen geben, wie sie ihr eigenes Gewerbe auffassen, was sie an der Welt anders machen möchten, soweit es in ihrer Reichweite liegt. Und es die Bedingungen zulassen – die Größe und der Zuschnitt des Baugrundstücks, die finanziellen Mittel, die baurechtlichen, städtebaulichen, nachbarschaftsrechtlichen, feuerpolizeilichen und hundert andere Vorgaben.

»Ein existentielles Weltstück«

Oswald Mathias Ungers (1926–2007) war ein denkender Architekt, ein *architectus doctus*. So ist es kein Wunder, daß er sich auch mit dem Bau eines eigenen Hauses theoretisch auseinander gesetzt hat. Das Haus war für ihn »Lebensraum«, »Laboratorium«, »die Summe der Erkenntnisse und Erfahrungen«, »ein kleines Universum«, »ein existentielles Weltstück«.[1] Es muß mit diesem hohen Anspruch zusammenhängen, daß er behaupten konnte, nichts sei quälender, als im eigenen Haus wohnen zu müssen. Also stand nicht das Glück der Selbstverwirklichung auf der Rechnung, sondern der ständige Zweifel, was er anders hätte machen können, sollen, müssen?

Drei Häuser hat Ungers im Laufe seines Lebens für sich selbst und seine Familie gebaut, zwei in Köln-Müngersdorf, eines in der Eifel.[2] Je nach Anlaß und Gelegenheit hat er in ihnen gelebt und gearbeitet – als sie alle drei gebaut waren, auch gleichzeitig. Warum, fragte er sich und seine Leser, sollte ein Architekt drei Häuser für sich bauen, wenn es schon schwierig genug sei, in einem einzigen eigenen Haus zu wohnen? Er habe lange Zeit gelitten in seinem ersten Haus, jeden Tag, jeden Morgen nach dem Aufstehen. Immer wieder, tausendmal habe er das Haus theoretisch umgezeichnet und darüber gegrübelt, was er anders, besser hätte machen können.[3]

Andere Architekten, die sich ein eigenes Haus gebaut haben, wurden nicht von solchen Skrupeln heimgesucht. In der Tat haben Ungers' Bedenken etwas Luxuriöses angesichts der Menschen, die nicht in einem eigenen Haus, geschweige denn in dreien leben können! Bei zahlreichen Kollegen in Vergangenheit und Gegenwart war es die Veränderung der Lebensumstände, die sie zu Neubauten auf eigene Rechnung zwang: Ortswechsel in eine andere Stadt, Berufung an eine neue Hochschule, und im Jahrhundert der Emigrationen: Flucht und Vertreibung. Walter Gropius, Ernst May, Erich Mendelsohn, Bruno Taut, Henry van de Velde haben sich nicht freiwillig auf einen Neuanfang eingelassen und ihre heimischen Domizile aufgegeben. Sie waren gezwungen, sich eine neue Existenz aufzubauen, und wenn sie Glück hatten, gehörte auch ein neues Haus dazu.

Der Fall Ungers liegt anders. Auch hat Ungers in den 1960er Jahren zeitweise seinen Lebensmittelpunkt von Köln weg verlagert, als er an die Technische Hochschule (heute: Universität) Berlin geholt wurde und dann Berufungen an nordamerikanische Universitäten annahm.[4] Diese Ortswechsel führten aber zu keinen Hausbauten. In seiner Berliner Zeit erwarb er im Westend ein Wohnhaus aus den frühen 1920er Jahren, einen hell verputzten Beinahe-Kubus, der fast von ihm selbst aus seinen späteren Jahren hätte stammen können.[5] Daß Ungers sich mehrfach auf das Abenteuer eines privaten Hausbaus einließ, hing vielmehr mit dem Wunsch zusammen, die Möglichkeiten seines jeweiligen, sich ändernden Repertoires zu erproben. Eigene Häuser zu bauen, bedeutete für Ungers, angewandte Hausbauforschung zu betreiben und der Mitwelt seine Vorstellung eines Hauses mitzuteilen.

Und weil ein Haus für Ungers nicht nur Bedarfsbefriedigung war, sondern Erwerb räumlicher Erfahrungen und Erprobung des Möglichen, ja weil es ihm dabei um Prinzipien der Architektur ging, war auch seine Leidensanfälligkeit entsprechend groß. »Das Haus ist ein Abbild der Idee von Welt, von Leben, von Existenz.« Wer so hoch setzt, nimmt Enttäuschungen nicht leicht – auch wenn ein wenig Koketterie bei seinen Unmutsbekundungen mitgespielt haben dürfte. Immerhin verzeichnete Ungers auch positive Gemütszustände. »Manchmal war ich glücklich und begeistert vom Ambiente und fühlte mich geborgen«, schrieb er über das Leben im Haus an der Belvederestraße.[6] Aber: »manchmal« ist nicht immer.

In der Architekturgeschichte finden sich unter den Architekten, die ein Wohnhaus oder gar mehrere Wohnhäuser für sich selbst bauten, auch solche, die ihrem späten Nachfahren Ungers an Experimentierlust gleichkamen oder ihn übertrafen. Eine Motivation für gebildete Baukünstler, eigene Häuser zu errichten, war es seit Renaissance und Manierismus, der Mit- und Nachwelt den erreichten gesellschaftlichen Status des Architekten bekannt zu machen. *Per lasciare memoria di sé*, formulierte der toskanische Universalkünstler und Biograph Giorgio Vasari (1511–1574) in seinem Raffael-Kapitel, habe der Malerarchitekt sich einen Palazzo in Rom, im Borgo Nuovo, errichtet.[7] Zu dem inneren Beweggrund, die Möglichkeiten ihrer Profession auszuloten, kam der sozusagen externe, durch repräsentative Wohnstätten das Verhältnis des Künstlers zur sozialen Außenwelt zu definieren. An der Repräsentation maß sich die Repräsentanz, die dem Künstler zugebilligt wurde. Sie war, versteht sich, immer auch an künftige Auftraggeber an den Fürstenhöfen und im gehobenen Bürgertum adressiert.[8]

Voraussetzung war, daß nicht allein mehr die Tradition und damit die Selbstverständlichkeit des Handelns galt. Wahlmöglichkeiten taten sich auf und wurden wahrgenommen, zumeist innerhalb der Grenzen des stilistisch Erlaubten und Angesagten, aber zunehmend – vor allem seit dem 19. Jahrhundert – mit gezielt innovatorischem Programm. So zeichnet sich auch in Ungers' Werk, nicht zuletzt in seinen eigenen Hausbauten, eine Abfolge unterschiedlicher, aber sich auseinander ergebender Haltungen ab. Das Haus in der Belvederestraße in Köln-Müngersdorf (1958–59) war der mauerstark-kraftvolle Auftritt eines jungen Architekten, der wirkte und wirken sollte. Das zweite Wohnhaus, das Ungers sich selber leistete, das Haus Glashütte (1986–88), war ein prototypisches Satteldachhaus in einem idyllischen Waldtal der Eifel. Strenge der Architektur stand gegen Freiheit der Natur. Ungers wählte seine *villeggiatura* dort, wo auch Römer ihre Landhäuser hatten.[9] Das dritte, letzte Haus am Kämpchensweg (1994–96), nur ein paar Schritte

1. Oswald Mathias Ungers, 2003. (Photo: Peter H. Fürst.)
2. Oswald Mathias Ungers, Haus Belvederestraße 60, Köln-Müngersdorf, 1958/59. Zustand 1960. (Photo: Walter Ehmann.)
3. Oswald Mathias Ungers, Haus Glashütte, bei Utscheid, Eifel, 1986–88. (Photo: Stefan Müller.)
4. Oswald Mathias Ungers, Haus Kämpchensweg 58, Köln-Müngersdorf, 1994/95. (Photo: Stefan Müller.)

1. Oswald Mathias Ungers, 2003. (Photo: Peter H. Fürst.)
2. Oswald Mathias Ungers, Haus Belvederestraße 60, Müngersdorf, Cologne, 1958/59. State in 1960. (Photo: Walter Ehmann.)
3. Oswald Mathias Ungers, Haus Glashütte, near Utscheid, Eifel, 1986–88. (Photo: Stefan Müller.)
4. Oswald Mathias Ungers, Haus Kämpchensweg 58, Müngersdorf, Cologne, 1994/95. (Photo: Stefan Müller.)

Wolfgang Pehnt

Haus Belvederestraße 60, Müngersdorf, Cologne

When architects build a house for themselves, one would think they are fulfilling a career aspiration. They are able to apply what they have learned. There is no client to raise objections, for they themselves are the clients. They can choose the form and the ground plan they believe most corresponds with their own and their families' ideas, behaviour patterns and housing needs. They can show others how they conceive of their own profession, what it is they would like to change about the world as far as lies within their capacity. And as far as conditions permit – the size and shape of the building site, financial resources, building permits, urban planning legislation, neighbour law, fire safety rules and a hundred other regulations.

»An existential piece of world«

Oswald Mathias Ungers (1926–2007) was a thinking architect, an *architectus doctus*. It is therefore no wonder he also had a theoretical approach to the building of his own house. For him the house was »a habitat«, »a laboratory«, »the sum of insights and experience«, »a little universe«, »an existential piece of world«.[1] No doubt because he had such high standards he used to claim that nothing was more excruciating than having to live in one's own house. In other words, he was not granted the happiness of self-fulfilment, but constant doubt: what could he, should he, ought he to have done differently?

In the course of his life, Ungers built himself and his family three houses, two in Müngersdorf, Cologne, one in the Eifel highlands.[2] Depending on the occasion and circumstances he lived and worked in them – often at the same time, once all three of them had been built. Why, he asked himself and his readers, should an architect build three houses for himself if it was already difficult enough to live in one single house of his own? He had suffered for a long time in his first house, he said – every day, every morning after getting up. Again and again, a thousand times over, he said, he had theoretically redrawn the house and pondered what he could have done differently, better.[3]

Other architects who have built their own house were not affected by such scruples. Indeed, there is something luxurious about Ungers' reservations given that there are people who are not able to live in a house of their own, let alone three of them! Many colleagues in the past and present were forced to build a new home at their own expense by a change of circumstances: a move to a different city, an appointment at another university and, in the century of emigrations: flight and exile. Walter Gropius, Ernst May, Erich Mendelsohn, Bruno Taut, Henry van de Velde did not voluntarily embrace a fresh start and give up their native domiciles. They were compelled to build a new existence, and if they were lucky, this included a new house.

In Ungers' case the situation was different. In the 1960s, he too intermittently relocated the central point of his life away from Cologne when he was invited to teach at the Technische Hochschule (now: Universität) Berlin and later accepted appointments at North American universities.[4] But these moves did not result in his building new houses. While in Berlin, he purchased an early-1920s residence in Westend, a brightly plastered quasi-cube he might easily have designed himself in his later years.[5] The fact that Ungers repeatedly embarked on the adventure of building his own private house had more to do with his wish to explore the possibilities of his repertoire at the time – a repertoire that kept changing. For Ungers, building his own houses meant doing research in applied house construction and sharing his concept of a house with his contemporaries.

And because a house allowed Ungers not only to satisfy a need, but rather to acquire spatial experience and explore what was possible – indeed, because he was concerned with the principles of architecture, the experience was just as painful as it was pleasurable. »A house is a representation of the idea of the world, of life, of existence.« A man whose stakes are so high does not take disappointments lightly – even though there might have been a hint of coquetry about his expressions of dissatisfaction. At any rate, Ungers also recorded positive feelings. »Sometimes I was happy and enthusiastic about the ambience and felt safe and secure«, he wrote about life in the Belvedere house.[6] However: »sometimes« is not always.

In architecture history, among the architects who built a residential house or even several houses for their personal use, there are some whose pleasure in experimenting rivalled that of their late successor Ungers or even excelled it. Ever since the Renaissance and mannerism, one motivation for trained architects for building their own homes has been to proclaim to his contemporaries and to posterity the social status the architect has attained. In his chapter about Raphael, the Tuscan universal artist and biographer Giorgio Vasari (1511–1574) wrote that the painter and architect had built a palazzo in Rome, in the Borgo Nuovo, *per lasciare memoria di sé*.[7] Added to the inner motive – to explore all the potentials of their profession – there was the external one, so to speak: to define, by means of representative residences, the relation of the artist to the social outside world. Representation was a gauge of the representative capability accorded to the artist. And, it goes without saying, it was always directed at future patrons at princely courts and in the upper echelons of the middle class.[8]

The assumption was that it was no longer tradition alone, and thus self-evident action, that counted. New options appeared and were pursued; for the most part, these were within the boundaries of what was stylistically permitted and fashionable, but increasingly – particularly since the 19th century – they had a specific innovative programme. Thus Ungers' work, too, including the houses he built for himself, is characterised by a succession of positions that, while different from one another, evolve from each other. The house in Belvederestraße in Müngersdorf, Cologne (1958–59), expressed the strong, vigorous stance of a young architect who was effective and intended to be so. The second private home Ungers built for himself, the Glashütte House (1986–88), was a prototypical gable roof house in an idyllic wooded valley in the Eifel highlands. The severity of its architecture contrasted with the freedom of nature. Ungers chose to locate his *villeggiatura* where the Romans, too, had had their country houses.[9] The third, and last, house, on Kämpchensweg (1994–96), only a few steps from the first house, was a structure that almost hit the rock-bottom level of abstraction.

vom ersten Haus entfernt, war ein Gebilde fast am Nullpunkt der Abstraktion.

Experimentierort Architektenhaus

Die verschiedenen Aufgaben, die Ungers seinem Haus an der Belvederestraße auftrug, waren in Künstlerhäusern der Kunstgeschichte vorweggenommen. Exemplarisch erfüllt, ja übererfüllt waren sie in John Soanes Häusern an Lincoln's Inn Fields, London. Soane (1753–1837) war Sammler, Architekt und akademischer Lehrer, der sein Domizil als Privatmuseum, Experimentierort, Memorialbau verstand.[10] Nach immer neuen Erweiterungen und Zukäufen bestand dieses Gesamtkunstwerk schließlich aus drei miteinander verbundenen Gebäuden.[11] Das komplexe Gebilde wahrte mit seiner Fassade mühsam das Dekorum, bot aber innen ein *non plus ultra* an überbordender Phantasie, an unerwarteten Raumeffekten, museologischem Raffinement, an Büchern, Gemälden, Architekturmodellen, Kunstgewerbe und antiquarischen Fundstücken aller Zeiten.

Vergleichbar in der Verwendung der eigenen Wohnhäuser als Studienobjekten, exemplarischen Stationen stilistischen Wandels und gesellschaftlicher Statussymbolik waren die Bauten, die der österreichische Baukünstler Otto Wagner (1841–1918) für sich errichtete.[12] Wagner, Historist und dann Reformer, entwarf und realisierte auf eigene Rechnung nicht weniger als vier Wohnungen in selbst entworfenen Etagenhäusern, ein mehrstöckiges Wohnhaus in der Straßenflucht, am Rennweg in Wien III, und zwei Villen in Wien XIV. Die beiden Villen stehen in unmittelbarer Nachbarschaft zueinander. Ihr Nebeneinander wirkt wie die absichtsvolle Demonstration eines Entwicklungssprungs. Auf den Glamour eines Architektensitzes mit dem Pathos eines italienischen Renaissancepalais bei der ersten Villa folgten in der zweiten schräg gegenüber pragmatische Bescheidung und sparsamere Dekoration. Sie zeigen Wagner auf dem Wege zum »Nutzstil«.

Auch jetzt verzichtete Wagner nicht auf Kunst in der Bewältigung der Bauaufgabe. Aber mit der zweiten Villa betrat er den Weg einer künstlerischen Auseinandersetzung mit Technik und Utilität. Den Spruch Gottfried Sempers *artis sola domina necessitas* hatte er schon an der Außenseite der ersten Villa angebracht, ohne daß man bei dieser prächtig geschmückten, säulenverzierten Künstlerresidenz Notwendigkeit, *necessitas*, als »einzige Herrin der Kunst« erkennt. Die zweite Villa ein Vierteljahrhundert später läßt eher an Einschränkung und Rückzug denken. Sie kündigt eine neue Ästhetik der Bescheidung an: einfache Kastenform, Verzicht auf Symmetrie, Reihung der Räume in der oberen Etage und der Fenster in der Fassade, Dekoration nur durch flächige Elemente, Fliesenbänder und -felder, Glasplättchen, kleine Aluminiumscheiben.

Uns scheint auch der »Neustil« dieses Bauwerks noch fern jeder Zweckmäßigkeitsdoktrin zu stehen. Aber der Abstand zwischen den beiden Häusern, die in der Hüttelbergstraße der gleichzeitigen Betrachtung dargeboten werden, ist enorm. Der Impuls, sich eine neue Villa zu bauen, ist im Wandel der Architekturideale zu suchen. Denn an einem Mangel an Wagnerschem Immobilienbesitz kann es nicht gelegen haben. Man denkt an die Konfrontation von Ungers' Häusern in Köln-Müngersdorf. Auch sie scheinen – nur ein paar Schritte voneinander entfernt, wenn auch nicht gleichzeitig im Blick – zwei unterschiedlichen Formenwelten zu entstammen. Auch bei ihnen wird die räumliche Nähe zum demonstrativen Vergleich genutzt. Das letzte Haus am Kämpchensweg nannte Ungers »ein Haus ohne Eigenschaften«. Das frühe Haus an der Belvederestraße weist dagegen sehr viele Eigenschaften auf – wobei auch die angebliche Eigenschaftslosigkeit des späteren Hauses als sehr deutlich ausgeprägte Eigenschaft gelten muß.

Beginn einer Karriere

Als Oswald Mathias Ungers sein erstes eigenes Wohnhaus an der Belvederestraße entwarf, hatte er acht Jahre Berufspraxis hinter sich. Ungers stammte aus einfachen Verhältnissen. Geboren wurde er 1926 in Kaisersesch, einem kleinen Ort am Rand der Eifel, der 1321 von Ludwig dem Bayern (ab 1328 Kaiser) Stadtrechte erhalten hatte. Der Bestandteil »Kaiser« im Ortsnamen rührt daher. Als der Vater Postbeamter in Mayen wurde, zog die Familie in das etwas größere Eifelstädtchen Mayen um. Erinnerungen an die Römerzeit finden sich in beiden Orten, die an der Römerstraße zwischen Trier und Andernach lagen. In Mayen besuchte Ungers das Realgymnasium. In der Nähe liegt das Benediktinerkloster Maria Laach, wo der junge Ungers bei Bauforschungen half. In Maria Laach erfuhr er nicht nur die Gesetzmäßigkeit einer großen mittelalterlichen Bauanlage, sondern auch die strengen Rituale des Ordenslebens mit seiner festgelegten Tagzeitenliturgie.

Das Architekturstudium absolvierte Ungers im Geschwindmarsch, innerhalb von drei Jahren. Er ging 1947 an die Technische Hochschule (heute: Universität) Karlsruhe, die dank ihrer Dozenten Otto Haupt, Otto Ernst Schweizer und vor allem Egon Eiermann (1904–1970) in der Architektenausbildung zu den angesehensten Hochschulen der Bundesrepublik zählte. Ungers schrieb sich bei Eiermann ein, der ein burschikoser und brillanter Redner war, über aktuelle Informationen aus der Welt der westlichen Moderne verfügte und seine Studenten makelloses Handwerk und Präzision im Detail lehrte. Monumentalität, überhaupt der Vorrang der Form war tabu. »Die gute Funktion eines Hauses hängt im wesentlichen davon ab, daß der darin arbeitende Mensch funktioniert, das heißt, daß er die Arbeit, die er zu seiner und seiner Familie Ernährung, aber nicht freiwillig leistet, möglichst fröhlich tut. Fröhlichkeit zu vermitteln, gehört eben auch zur guten Funktion eines Hauses.«[13]

In seinen eigenen Bauten setzte Eiermann auf den klaren, aristokratischen Stahl im Gegensatz zum Gemisch des – in seinen Augen – plebejischen Betons, der erst durch Schalung Form erhält. Tragen und Lasten werden in nachvollziehbaren Verbindungen dargestellt. Vor den Traggerüsten liegt eine Schicht sekundärer Elemente wie Laufgänge für Reinigung, Reparatur und Feuerbekämpfung, Fluchtwege, Nottreppenhäuser, starrer oder beweglicher Sonnenschutz, Rankgitter für Begrünung. Das Gestänge solcher Umgänge legt eine Zone zwischen Innen- und Außenraum und bildet eine filigrane Fassadengraphik. Den oft beträchtlichen Bauvolumen, mit denen es Eiermann zu tun hatte, nimmt sie den Eindruck der Massigkeit, suggeriert Leichtigkeit, Transparenz und »Fröhlichkeit«.

Das ist nicht der Weg, den Ungers einschlagen wird. Vor allem vermißte der junge Architekt bei Eiermann Begründungen, die über die sachgerechte Konstruktion, die Sicherheit in der Materialwahl und die Disziplin der

5. Sir John Soane, Häuser Lincoln's Inn Fields 12–14, London, 1792–1824. Der Bereich mit der Kuppel. (Photo: Richard Bryant.)
6. Otto Wagner, Villa I, Hüttelbergstaße 26, Wien XIV, 1886–88. (Photo: Welleschik.)
7. Otto Wagner, Villa II, Hüttelbergstraße 28, Wien XIV, 1912/13. (Photo: Müsse.)

5. Sir John Soane, Houses Lincoln's Inn Fields 12–14, London, 1792–1824. The space with the dome. (Photo: Richard Bryant.)
6. Otto Wagner, Villa I, Hüttelbergstraße 26, Wien XIV, 1886–88. (Photo: Welleschik.)
7. Otto Wagner, Villa II, Hüttelbergstraße 28, Wien XIV, 1912/13. (Photo: Müsse.)

The architect's house – a place for experimentation

The various functions Ungers assigned to his Belvederestraße house had been anticipated in artist houses throughout history. In an exemplary manner, they had been fulfilled, indeed over-fulfilled, in John Soane's houses at Lincoln's Inn Fields, London. Soane (1753 to 1837) was a collector, architect and academic teacher who saw his domicile as a private museum, a place for experimentation, a memorial.[10] After repeated expansions and additional acquisitions, this all-encompassing work of art eventually consisted of three connected buildings.[11] The complex structure observed the proprieties with difficulty as far as the façade was concerned, but its interior was the ultimate in exuberant fantasy, unexpected spatial effects, museological refinement, books, paintings, architectural models, arts and crafts, and antiquarian finds of all time.

The homes that Austrian architect Otto Wagner (1841 to 1918) built for himself were comparable: Wagner used his own residences as objects of study, exemplary stages of stylistic change and symbolism of social status.[12] Wagner, a historicist and subsequently a reformer, designed and implemented no less than four apartments at his own expense in multi-floor buildings he designed himself, a multi-storey home in alignment with other buildings in the 3d District of Vienna, and two villas in the 14th District of Vienna. The two villas are immediately adjacent to each other. The effect of this is like the intentional demonstration of a developmental leap. The glamour of an architect's residence that had the dramatic effect of an Italian Renaissance palace, in the first villa, was followed in the second, diagonally opposite, by pragmatic unpretentiousness and more sparing decoration. They show Wagner moving toward a functional style (»Nutzstil«).

Here too, Wagner did not dispense with art as he approached the task of building. But the second villa was his way of addressing technology and utility as an artist. He had already mounted Gottfried Semper's maxim *artis sola domina necessitas* on the exterior wall of the first villa, though it is difficult to recognise necessity, *necessitas*, as the »sole mistress of art« in this sumptuously decorated artist's residence with its splendid columns. The second villa, a quarter century later, is more likely to make one think of restraint and withdrawal. It proclaims a new aesthetics of unpretentiousness: a simple box shape, the absence of symmetry, the serial arrangement of rooms on the top floor and of windows in the façade, decoration only with two-dimensional elements, strips and panels of tiles, little glass slabs, small aluminium discs.

To us, even the »New Style« (»Neustil«) of this building still seems far removed from any doctrine of functionality. But the distance between the two houses, on simultaneous display in Hüttelbergstraße, is enormous. Wagner's impulse to build himself a new villa is due to changing ideals in architecture. For Wagner can hardly have suffered from a lack of real estate properties. We are reminded of the confrontation of Ungers' houses in Müngersdorf, Cologne. They too – merely a few steps from each other, even though not simultaneously in sight – seem to have evolved from two different stylistic worlds. Here too their close proximity is used for the purpose of demonstrative comparison. Ungers called the last house on Kämpchensweg »a house without qualities«. The early house in Belvederestraße, on the other hand, has quite a lot of qualities – but the alleged lack of qualities of the later house must be considered a very pronounced quality, too.

The beginning of a career

When Oswald Mathias Ungers designed his first personal residence on Belvederestraße, he had been in professional practice for eight years. Ungers came from a humble background. He was born in 1926 in Kaisersesch, a small town on the periphery of the Eifel mountains that had received its town charter in 1321 from Ludwig the Bavarian (who became Holy Roman emperor in 1328), hence the word »Kaiser« in the name of the town. When Ungers' father became a postal clerk in Mayen, the family moved to the somewhat larger Eifel town of Mayen. Reminders of Roman times can be found in both towns, which were located on the Roman road leading from Trier to Andernach. In Mayen Ungers attended secondary school. Not far from Mayen is the Benedictine monastery of Maria Laach, where young Ungers helped with building research. In Maria Laach he not only learned about the laws governing a large medieval building complex, but at the same time about the strict rituals of monastic life with its fixed Liturgy of the Hours.

Ungers completed his architecture studies at an accelerated pace, within three years. In 1947 he enrolled at the Technische Hochschule (now: Universität) Karlsruhe, which thanks to its lecturers Otto Haupt, Otto Ernst Schweizer and above all Egon Eiermann (1904 to 1970) was considered to be one of the most renowned colleges in the Federal Republic of Germany in the field of architectural education. Ungers signed up for Eiermann's course. The latter was a laid-back and brilliant speaker, had the latest information from the world of Western Modernism, and taught his students flawless craft and precision in detail. Monumentality was taboo, as was any prioritising of form. »The good function of a house essentially depends on the fact that the person who works in it is functioning, in other words, that he does the work he performs in order to feed himself and his family, though not voluntarily chosen, as joyfully as possible. Giving a sense of joy, you see, is also part of the good function of a house.«[13]

In his own buildings Eiermann preferred clear, aristocratic steel as opposed to the conglomeration of – as he saw it – plebeian concrete, which is only given its form by shuttering. Supports and weights are represented in easily understandable relationships. In front of the supporting framework there is a layer of secondary elements such as walkways for cleaning, repairs and firefighting, escape routes, emergency stairwells, rigid or mobile sun protection, trellises for climbing plants. Such passageways create a zone between the interior and exterior and produce a filigree façade pattern. In the often huge buildings Eiermann worked on, this zone takes away the impression of massiveness, suggesting lightness, transparency and »joy«.

That is not the path Ungers was to follow. What the young architect missed in Eiermann above all were rationales that went beyond proper construction, safety in the choice of materials, and discipline of means. It was impossible to speak to Eiermann, as Ungers experienced him, about architecture as an art form and about

Mittel hinausgingen. Über den Kunstcharakter und die zeitüberdauernden Ideen im Bauen war mit Eiermann, wie Ungers ihn erlebte, nicht zu reden, eher schon mit Schweizer oder dem Karlsruher Bauforscher Karl Wulzinger.[14] Seine übrigen Gesprächspartner suchte der junge Ungers sich, wo er mit einem von Kunstwillen, bildhaftem Denken und organischen Lebensvorgängen geprägten Architekturverständnis rechnen konnte: Hugo Häring (1882–1958) etwa, den er in dessen Wohnort Biberach aufsuchte, und Rudolf Schwarz (1897–1961), den Kirchenbauer und Kölner Stadtplaner. Zu ihm stellte sich in Müngersdorf ein distanziert-nachbarschaftliches Verhältnis her, das auf gegenseitiger Wertschätzung beruhte.[15]

Ungers sorgte dafür, daß sein Bildungsweg nicht nur in der deutschen Szene verlief. Auf der IX.Tagung der CIAM, der Congrès Internationaux d' Architecture Moderne, in Aix-en-Provence 1953 erlebte er die Auseinandersetzungen einer jüngeren Generation mit den Heroen der rationalistischen Architekturmoderne, die zur Gründung des oppositionellen Team X führte.[16] Gern erzählte Ungers die Geschichte, wie der temperamentvolle niederländische Architekt Aldo van Eyck (1918–99) eine Rotweinflasche in die Richtung von Walter Gropius warf, als der Patriarch allzu seigneural und unberührt von den Problemen des aktuellen Massenzeitalters auftrat.[17] 1954 besuchte Ungers – zusammen mit seinem Kommilitonen und Freund Reinhard Gieselmann (1925–2013) – die Biennale in Venedig und die Triennale in Mailand. Über Mailand berichteten beide in einem gemeinsamen Artikel und stellten ein »Gefühl der Zusammengehörigkeit des heutigen Formschaffens« fest.[18]

Die ersten Bauten, die Ungers unter seinem Namen veröffentlichen ließ, entstanden in einer Bürogemeinschaft mit dem Architekten Helmut Goldschmidt (1918–2005). Sie bestand bis Anfang des Jahres 1955. Das Büro firmierte als Goldschmidt & Ungers. Goldschmidt, acht Jahre älter als Ungers, hatte Aufträge und baute unter anderem die Kölner Synagoge an der Roonstraße wieder auf. Wie Ungers stammte er aus Mayen. Bevor Goldschmidt nach Köln übersiedelte, führte er dort ein Büro, in dem Ungers während seiner Studienzeit sein Praktikum absolvierte.[19] Mehrgeschossige Häuser in Baulücken, die Ungers in seiner Goldschmidt-Epoche errichtete, sind Putzbauten. Auf den zweiten Blick zeichnen sie sich durch gediegene, rhythmisierte Fassadenlösungen auf. Symmetrie wird mit subtilen Abweichungen unterlaufen, die Disziplin der Straßenfront aber gewahrt.[20] An die Konventionen der damaligen Moderne hielt sich der Eiermann-Schüler noch.

Nach der Trennung von Goldschmidt ändert sich das. Die Mehrfamilienhäuser, die Ungers jetzt baut, sind gestaffelt, fangen Licht und bilden Schatten. Sie zeigen unverhüllt das Baumaterial, Ziegel und Betonstürze. Fenster werden um die Gebäudekanten geführt. Kaminschlote setzen plastische Akzente. Einige Male handelt es sich um größere Komplexe, die sich in Ketten und Höfen organisieren. Grundrisse mit vor- und zurücktretenden Risaliten, Balkons und Loggien fördern die Gruppenbildung der Anlagen. Es entsteht der Eindruck einer kraftvollen, dynamischen Architektur, den Ungers auch auf innerstädtische Bauten in der Straßenflucht übertrug. Aus dieser Periode stammt auch ein anspruchsvolles Zweifamilienhaus in Köln-Hohenlind, das Haus Müller, das sich aus mehreren, allerdings noch in weißem Rauputz gehaltenen Baukörpern zusammensetzt. Im Wechsel positiver und negativer Volumen – darunter auch Zylinderformen für Treppenhäuser und Kaminplatz – zeichnet sich bereits das Konzept eines Hauses als kleiner Stadt ab, das dann für das eigene Wohnhaus in Müngersdorf zutrifft.[21]

Ein Haus als Manifest

Architekten bauten damals, wenn sie eigene Häuser realisierten, in der Regel frei stehende Bungalows – und tun es wohl auch heute noch. Dagegen erwarb Ungers für seinen geplanten Neubau ein Grundstück in einer Ortslage, Müngersdorf. Der dörfliche Vorort im Westen Kölns liegt an der Aachener Straße, der einstigen Via Belgica, am Übergang der Niederterrasse des Rheintals zur Mittelterrasse. Gräberfelder und ein römischer Gutshof sind ergraben worden. Nahe römischer Vergangenheit konnte sich Ungers auch hier am richtigen Ort fühlen. In unmittelbarer Nähe befindet sich der Stadtwald. Eine privilegierte Situation also, historisch wie topographisch. Vom Wald und seinen Wiesen machten Herr, Frau und Hund bei Spaziergängen gern Gebrauch.

Das Baugrundstück und damit auch der Neubau schließt eine – damals noch nicht zur Gänze bebaute – Zeile von Reihenhäusern ab. Mit dem unmittelbar angrenzenden Nachbarhaus Belvederestraße Nr.58 teilt das Haus Ungers (Nr. 60) ein Stück des durchlaufenden Satteldachs, das aber nach wenigen Metern im Ungersschen Bereich abgewalmt ist. Immerhin deckt das ziegelgedeckte Dach noch die vortretende Mauerstirn des ersten Obergeschosses im rechten Hausteil. Rücksichtnahme gehörte zum inhaltlichen Programm. Die isolierten Fenstergauben der Nachbarn werden auf der Ungers-Seite zu einem lang gezogenen Fensterband.

»Dichte« war eine in den 1960/70er Jahren viel diskutierte Forderung, die zur nicht minder erwünschten »Urbanität« gehörte. Urbanität hieß die Alternative zum funktionalistischen Städtebau der Moderne, der getreu der Maximen der *Charta von Athen* in Funktionen aufgeteilt und zergliedert worden war.[22] Der Begriff Urbanität dagegen verband sich mit Überlagerung, Mischung, Verflechtung.[23] Hier wurde er vom Städtebau auf den Hausbau übertragen. Der Slogan vom Haus als kleiner Stadt (*minima civitas*) und von der Stadt als großem Haus (*maxima domus*), der seit Alberti die europäische Architekturgeschichte durchzieht,[24] gilt auch für diesen Bau, für diesen Bau erst recht. In seiner ersten großen Monographie überschrieb Ungers ein Kapitel mit »Das Haus als Abbild der Stadt«.[25]

Infolgedessen waren der Baumeister, seine Frau Liselotte (»Lo«), ihre drei Kinder Simon, Sibylle und Sophia, ihre Katzen und Hunde nicht die einzigen Nutzer des Hauses. Das Haus diente nicht nur als Wohnhaus, sondern auch als Architektenbüro für den Chef und seine Mitarbeiter, als Besprechungsort, als Bibliothek und Ort der Kunstsammlung. Der Hausteil rechts vom Eingang an der Belvederestraße enthielt im Erdgeschoß und im ersten Obergeschoß zunächst zwei Einliegerwohnungen mit jeweils zwei Räumen, Küche und Bad. Im Laufe der Zeit wurden diese Appartements ins Ganze einbezogen. Aber zunächst trugen die Mieteinnahmen zur Finanzierung des Hausbaus bei. Beide Wohnungen wurden über ein doppelläufiges Treppenhaus erschlossen, während die privaten Räume in der Hälfte des ersten und im ganzen zweiten Obergeschoß durch eine unabhängig davon geführte Wendeltreppe aus Terrazzo-Elementen bedient wurden. Die Hausteile konnten daher unabhän-

8. Egon Eiermann, Haus Eiermann, Krippenhof 16 bis 18, Baden-Baden, 1959–62. (Photo: Horstheinz Neuendorff.)
9. Oswald Mathias Ungers, Mehrfamilienhaus und Kleiderfabrik in der Aachener Straße, Köln-Braunsfeld, 1951. (Photo: Hugo Schmölz.)
10. Oswald Mathias Ungers, Mehrfamilienhäuser in der Mauenheimer Straße, Köln-Nippes, 1957–59. (Photo: Walter Ehmann.)
11. Oswald Mathias Ungers, Zweifamilienhaus in der Werthmannstraße, Köln-Hohenlind, 1957/58. (Photo: Friedhelm Thomas.)

8. Egon Eiermann, Haus Eiermann, Krippenhof 16 to 18, Baden-Baden, 1959–62. (Photo: Horstheinz Neuendorff.)
9. Oswald Mathias Ungers, multi-family house und garment factory on Aachener Straße, Braunsfeld, Cologne, 1951. (Photo: Hugo Schmölz.)
10. Oswald Mathias Ungers, multi-family house on Mauenheimer Straße, Nippes, Cologne,1957–59. (Photo: Walter Ehmann.)
11. Oswald Mathias Ungers, two-family house on Werthmannstraße, Hohenlind, Cologne, 1957/58. (Photo: Friedhelm Thomas.)

enduring ideas in architecture; Ungers preferred to speak with Schweizer or the Karlsruhe building researcher Karl Wulzinger.[14] Young Ungers found the rest of his interlocutors wherever he could count on an understanding of architecture characterised by artistic intent, vivid thinking and organic life processes: for instance, Hugo Häring (1882–1958), whom he visited at his home in Biberach, and Rudolf Schwarz (1897–1961), a builder of churches and Cologne urban planner. With the latter, in Müngersdorf, he established a distant neighbourly relationship based on mutual esteem.[15]

Ungers saw to it that his education was not limited to the German scene. At the 9th conference of CIAM, the Congrès Internationaux d'Architecture Moderne, in Aix-en-Provence in 1953, he witnessed the clashes of a younger generation with the heroic figures of rationalistic Modernist architecture, which led to the founding of the opposition Team X.[16] Ungers enjoyed telling the story of how the temperamental Dutch architect Aldo van Eyck (1918–99) threw a bottle of red wine in the direction of Walter Gropius when the patriarch's demeanour was too lordly and unaffected by the problems of modern mass society.[17] In 1954 Ungers – together with his fellow student and friend Reinhard Gieselmann (1925–2013) – attended the Biennale in Venice and the Triennale in Milan. In a joint article, the two wrote a report about Milan, noting that there was a »feeling of solidarity among today's architects«.[18]

The first buildings Ungers published under his name were designed in an office he shared with the architect Helmut Goldschmidt (1918–2005). Their association continued until the early part of 1955. The office was registered under the name of Goldschmidt & Ungers. Goldschmidt, eight years older than Ungers, had commissions, including the rebuilding of the Cologne Synagogue in Roonstraße. Like Ungers, he was originally from Mayen. Before Goldschmidt moved to Cologne, he ran an office in Mayen in which Ungers did his internship while a student.[19] Multi-storey houses in gap sites built by Ungers in his Goldschmidt period are stucco buildings. At second glance they are characterised by sound rhythmic façade solutions. Symmetry is undermined by subtle deviations, though the discipline of the street façade has been preserved.[20] Eiermann's student still adhered to the conventions of the Modernism of his time.

This changed after his separation from Goldschmidt. The multifamily houses Ungers now built are staggered, catch the light and create shadows. They openly reveal the building material, bricks and concrete lintels. Windows are run around the edges of buildings. Chimneystacks provide three-dimensional accents. Sometimes Ungers designs larger complexes, organised into chains and courtyards. Ground plans with projections and recesses, balconies and loggias enhance the grouping of the buildings. This creates the impression of a powerful, dynamic architecture, an impression Ungers also conveyed in inner-city buildings that were part of the streetscape. During this period he also designed a sophisticated two-family house in Hohenlind, Cologne, the Müller House, composed of several structures, though still featuring white stucco. In the alternation of positive and negative volumes – including cylinder shapes for stairwells and fireplace – we can already see the concept of a house as a small town, which then applied to his own home in Müngersdorf.[21]

A house as a manifesto

At the time, architects normally used to build freestanding bungalows when building their own homes – and are no doubt still doing so to this day. Ungers, on the other hand, purchased a piece of land in the village of Müngersdorf for his projected new building. The rural suburb on the west side of Cologne is located on Aachener Straße, the former Via Belgica, where the lower terrace of the Rhine Valley transitions into the middle terrace. Burial grounds and a Roman country estate have been excavated here. Close to the Roman past, Ungers was again able to feel he was in the right place. Nearby is the town forest. In other words, this was a privileged situation, both historically and topographically. Master, mistress and dog enjoyed their walks in the woods and the surrounding meadows.

The building site and thus the new building as well are at the end of a line of row houses that had not been completely built up at the time. The Ungers House (no. 60) and the neighbour's house immediately next to it, Belvederestraße no. 58, share part of the continuous gable roof, which, however, is hipped after a few meters in the Ungers section. At any rate, the tiled roof still covers the projecting outer face of the first floor on the right side of the house. Consideration for one's neighbours was part of the programme. The neighbours' isolated dormer windows become a long row of windows on Ungers' side.

»Density« was a requirement, much discussed in the 1960s and '70s, that was part of a no less desirable »urbanity«. Urbanity was the alternative to the functionalist urban planning of the Modernist movement, which, true to the maxims of the *Athens Charter*, had been subdivided and dismembered into functions.[22] The term urbanity, on the other hand, was associated with overlaying, mixing, interweaving.[23] Here it was transferred from urban development to housing construction. The slogan that describes the house as a small town (*minima civitas*) and the town as a large house (*maxima domus*), which has been running like a thread through the history of European architecture since Alberti,[24] also applies to this building, and particularly this building. In his first major monograph, Ungers titled one chapter »The house as an image of the town«.[25]

Consequently, the architect, his wife Liselotte (»Lo«), their three children Simon, Sibylle and Sophia, and their cats and dogs were not the only users of the house. The house served not only as a residence, but also as an architect's office for the boss and his staff, as a meeting place, as a library and site of the art collection. The part of the house to the right of the Belvederestraße entrance initially contained, on the ground floor and the first floor, two two-room granny flats with kitchen and bathroom. As time went by, these apartments were integrated in the rest of the house. But at first the rental income contributed to the financing of the construction. Both flats were accessed by a double-flight stairwell, while the private rooms in one half of the first floor and in the entire second floor could be reached by an independent spiral terrazzo staircase. That is why the parts of the house could be used independently of each other. They even had walled gardens, each of which was accessible separately from the rest of the house – the garden of the architect's apartment on the top floor by a steep outside staircase along a strikingly stepped brick wall.

gig voneinander benutzt werden. Sie besaßen sogar ummauerte Gärten, die jeweils getrennt vom übrigen Ensemble aus zugänglich waren – der Garten der Architektenwohnung im Obergeschoß über eine steile Außentreppe entlang einer markant abgetreppten Backsteinwand.

In seinen *Aphorismen zum Häuserbauen* hat Ungers die Überschneidungen der Zwecke und Tätigkeiten genüßlich beschrieben. »Wir hatten das klassische *grocery-store arrangement*: Das Haus war der Laden, die Werkstatt, oben wurde gewohnt, wurden die Produkte hergestellt und wurde verhandelt. Dazwischen die Kinder und die Tiere ... Oben auf dem Söller wurden Vorlesungen geschrieben, unten im Keller Modelle gebaut. Eine kleine Welt für sich. Der Ammoniakduft von frischen Lichtpausen mischte sich mit den Kochdünsten der Küche. Alles unter einem Dach: Museumsstücke, wertvolle Bücher, Kinderrasseln und Futternäpfe.«[26] Ein wenig erinnert diese »kleine Welt« an das, was Kultursoziologen wie Wilhelm Heinrich Riehl (1823–97) einst als »das ganze Haus« der guten alten Zeit beschrieben haben: Wohnen und Arbeiten, Fremde wie Mitarbeiter in *einem* Bau, das Büro wie ein alter Handwerksbetrieb im Erdgeschoß.

Von einer Lichtkuppel bekrönt, zeichnet sich der Zylinder der »Privattreppe« bei geeignetem Standpunkt auch in der Außenansicht ab. Es ist gewissermaßen die Achse, um die sich das Haus »dreht«. Wenn die Wendeltreppe das vertikale Zentrum des Hauses in seinem ursprünglichen Zustand bildet, so wirkt ein gepflasterter Weg als Achse in der Horizontalen. Er führte vom westlichen Vorplatz am Eingang von der Belvederestraße über einige Stufen ins Haus, durchschneidet die ganze Länge des Grundstücks nach Osten, läuft als Korridor erst durch das Haus (wo man dem Gehäuse der Treppenspirale ausweichen muß), dann zwischen den ummauerten, aber damals noch nicht überbauten Gärten hindurch. Es war sozusagen die Entwicklungsachse der *minima civitas*, an der Ungers später, 1989, den Kubus der Bibliothek anhängen konnte. Zugleich wirkt der Weg als ordnendes Moment in der Vielfalt der Kuben, Quader, Zylinder und Terrassen.

Ein weiterer Bereich an einem Flur parallel zum »langen Weg«, von ihm durch eine tragende Wand getrennt, war dem Atelierbetrieb gewidmet, mit zwei Büros, einem Raum für mehrere Zeichentische und einem Besprechungsraum in einer Rotunde. Wie der Treppenzylinder empfängt sie Oberlicht durch eine Deckenkuppel. Außen läßt sie sparsamen Raum für ein weiteres Gärtchen, um das eine Außenmauer schwingt. Nimmt man hinzu, daß die Backsteinverbände der Haus- und Umfassungsmauern von Rollschichten gegliedert werden, daß dort, wo Mauern nicht recht-, sondern schiefwinklig aufeinander treffen, die Steine nicht abgeschlagen, sondern durchgesteckt wurden und einen nahezu textilen Saum bilden, daß die Höhe der Betonstürze entsprechend der Länge, über die sie sich erstrecken, wechselt, daß schließlich das weiß gestrichene Sprossenwerk der Stahlfenster und -Türen vor den späteren Dämmungs- und Lärmschutzmaßnahmen tief hinter den Außenwänden zurücklag, so wird einsichtig, wie ganz und gar plastisch diese Hausgruppe gedacht war. Das kompakte und – für ein Wohnhaus – vielteilige Programm führte zu einem Katarakt von Formen, der hier, am Ende der Häuserzeile, ausgeschüttet wurde. Licht und Schatten veranstalteten ihre Spiele auf den vor- und zurücktretenden Flächen des Bauwerks.

Es war ein Haus, in dem ein noch junger Architekt verdeutlichte, was er anders machen wollte als die Kollegen. Das Haus »zeigt alles, was ich damals konnte, läßt keine Möglichkeit aus: Sockel, Wand, Dach, Gesims, Leibung, schwere Materialität, Leichtigkeit, schwebende Abläufe, Brüche, unten Basis, oben Offenheit, soviel wie möglich.«[27] Auch abgesehen von Gestaltungsfragen war es ein aufwendiges Haus. In der ersten Fassung, vor dem Anbau der Bibliothek, hatte es eine Nutzfläche von 448 qm (ohne Kellergeschoß und Garage), nach der Erweiterung von 1990 740 qm.[28]

Ein paar Häuser weiter, am Lövenicher Weg, bewohnte Rudolf Schwarz sein Domizil. Der Vergleich zeigt den Unterschied der Generationen. Vier Jahre früher entstanden, ist das Haus des Kölner Stadtplaners und viel beschäftigten Baumeisters ein denkbar schlichtes, einstöckiges Backsteingebäude, wenn auch schön am Waldrand gelegen. Ein kleiner Büroflügel schließt im rechten Winkel an. Schwarz war noch von der Frugalität der Kriegs- und Nachkriegszeit geprägt und vertrat ein Ideal der »reinen und armen Gestalt«. Ungers dagegen entstammte einer jüngeren Generation, die ehrgeizig nach vorne drängte.[29] Bei der Finanzierung seines Hauses dürfte geholfen haben, daß Liselotte Ungers aus der begüterten Familie eines Wuppertaler Bauunternehmers stammte.

So willkürlich-subjektiv das Ungers-Haus damals manchem erscheinen mochte, es vertrat programmatische Forderungen. Körperhaft und räumlich sollte Architektur sein, erlebbar »durch Umschreiten und Eindringen«. Bewegung, Dynamik, Asymmetrie, Vitalität waren gefragt. Schöpferische Kunst – und um Kunst, Baukunst, ging es – müsse die bestehende Form zertrümmern, um den Ausdruck der eigenen Zeit zu finden. Bauen habe nicht dem Primat der Technik und der Gleichmacherei zu folgen. Jede wahre Schöpfung sei Kunst, und Architektur bedeutete für Ungers zumindest »partielle Schöpfung«. Diese Maxime war zugleich politisch verortet, nämlich »in einer lebendigen demokratischen Ordnung«, und kritisierte die »materialistischen Methoden« der zeitgenössischen Bauproduktion. »Freiheit lebt nur in der ständigen Auseinandersetzung des einzelnen mit der Realität und im Erkennen der persönlichen inneren Verantwortung gegenüber Ort, Zeit und Mensch.« »Einhüllung und Bergung« des Individuums werden als die Aufgabe, ja als das Wesen der Architektur gefordert.

Diese Zitate finden sich in einem Dokument, das kurz nach der Fertigstellung des Hauses entstand. Dessen Gedankengänge müssen aber ihre Verfasser auch bereits vorher beschäftigt haben. Es hatte zwei Autoren: Ungers und Reinhard Gieselmann. Beide waren Eiermann-Schüler, beide hatten ihre Vorbehalte gegenüber dem Meister. In den späten fünfziger und frühen sechziger Jahren sahen sie sich öfter, diskutierten, reisten gemeinsam nach Italien oder zu Le Corbusiers Kapelle in Ronchamp und verfaßten das Manifest *Zu einer neuen Architektur*.[30] Der Text wirkt ein wenig unorganisiert, wiederholt sich, kommt auf den Anfang zurück. So entsteht der Eindruck einer aus der Erregung der Stunde entstandenen Stellungnahme, in der es um nicht weniger als die »Erneuerung der europäischen Architektur« geht.

Die »Verantwortung gegenüber dem Ort«, die das Manifest anspricht, war auch konkret gemeint. Das Haus steht nicht an einer beliebigen Stelle, sondern an einem Ort, der den *genius loci* beherbergt, seinerseits

In his *Aphorismen zum Häuserbauen* (Aphorisms on building houses) Ungers described with obvious enjoyment the overlapping of functions and activities. »We had the classic *grocery-store arrangement*: The house was the store, the workshop, upstairs was where you lived, where products were manufactured, where arguments and negotiations took place. In between were the children and the animals ... Lectures were written upstairs on the balcony, models built down in the cellar. A little world of its own. The smell of ammonia of fresh blueprints mingled with the smells of cooking that came from the kitchen. Everything under one roof: museum pieces, valuable books, children's rattles and dog dishes.«[26] This »little world« is somewhat reminiscent of what cultural sociologists like Wilhelm Heinrich Riehl (1823–97) once described as »the complete house« of the good old days: living and working, strangers as well as staff in *one* building, the office on the ground floor like the business of an old-time craftsman.

Crowned by a domed roof-light, the cylinder of the »private staircase« can clearly be seen in the external view as well, from the right vantage point. It is, as it were, the axis around which the house »turns«. While the spiral staircase is the vertical centre of the house in its original condition, a paved path acts as an axis in the horizontal direction. This path led from the west forecourt at the Belvederestraße entrance up a few steps into the house, cuts through the entire length of the property eastward, runs as a corridor first through the house (where you have to avoid the casing of the spiral staircase), then through the walled gardens, which at the time had not yet been overbuilt. It was so to speak the development axis of the *minima civitas*, to which later, in 1989, Ungers was able to attach the cube of the library. At the same time, the path acts as a structuring factor in a multitude of cubes, cuboidal blocks, cylinders and terraces.

An additional area on a hallway parallel to the »long path«, separated from it by a load-bearing wall, was devoted to studio work, with two offices, a room for several drafting tables and a conference room in a rotunda. Like the cylindrical stairwell, it is lit from above by a ceiling cupola. Outside there is scant room for another tiny garden, which is surrounded by a curving exterior wall. Add to this the fact that the brick bonds of the house walls and enclosing walls are structured by brick-on-edge courses; that in places where the walls do not meet at 90 degrees but at an oblique angle, the stones were not chipped off but were inserted from front to back and form an almost textile seam; that the height of the concrete lintels changes in accordance with the length over which they extend; and finally that before later insulation and noise abatement measures were undertaken, the white painted sash bars of the steel windows and doors lay far behind the exterior walls, it is clear how very three-dimensional the design of this building was meant to be. The programme was compact and – for a residence – complex, producing a cataract of forms spilled here, at the end of the row of houses. Light and shadow played over the projecting and receding surfaces of the building complex.

It was a house in which a young architect demonstrated what he wanted to do differently from his colleagues. The house »shows everything I knew how to do at the time, leaves out no possibility: foundation, wall, roof, cornice, intrados, heavy materiality, lightness, suspended waste pipes, fractures, a base below, openness above, as much as possible.«[27] Even apart from questions of design it was a lavish house. In the first version, before the library was built on, it had a floor space of 448 square metres (without the basement and garage), and 740 square metres after the 1990 expansion.[28]

A few houses away, on Lövenicher Weg, Rudolf Schwarz had his home. A comparison shows the difference between the generations. Built four years earlier, the house of the Cologne urban planner and busy architect was a very simple one-storey brick building, though beautifully situated on the edge of a forest. There is a small office wing at a right angle to the house. The frugality of the war and postwar period had left its mark on Schwarz, who believed in the ideal of »pure and barren form«. Ungers, on the other hand, belonged to a younger generation that surged forward ambitiously.[29] When he financed his house, it probably helped that Liselotte Ungers came from the affluent family of a Wuppertal building contractor.

No matter how arbitrary and subjective the Ungers house may have appeared to some people at the time, it did represent programmatic claims. For architecture was supposed to be physical and spatial, to be experienced »by walking around it and penetrating it«. Movement, dynamism, asymmetry, vitality were in demand. Creative art – and architecture was an art form – must shatter existing form in order to find the expression of its own time. Building, it was claimed, did not need to follow the primacy of technology and egalitarianism. All true creation was art, and architecture for Ungers meant at least »partial creation«. At the same time this maxim was political in nature, rooted »in a living democratic order«, and criticised the »materialistic methods« of the contemporary construction industry. »We are free only insofar as we constantly confront reality and recognise our personal responsibility to place, time and human beings.« Ungers demands that the task, indeed the essence of architecture should be to »envelop and shelter« the individual.

These quotations are found in a document written shortly after the completion of the house. But the ideas contained in it must have preoccupied its authors even earlier. There were two of them: Ungers and Reinhard Gieselmann. Both were pupils of Eiermann, both had reservations regarding the master. In the late fifties and early sixties they saw each other frequently, engaged in discussions, travelled together to Italy or to Corbusier's chapel in Ronchamp and wrote the manifesto *Zu einer neuen Architektur* ("Towards a New Architecture").[30] The text seems somewhat disorganised, is repetitive, returns to the beginning. Thus one gets the impression that this was a position statement which arose from the excitement of the hour, concerned with no less than the »renewal of European architecture«.

The »responsibility toward the place« referred to in the manifesto was meant concretely as well. The house is not located at an arbitrary spot but in a place that houses the *genius loci*, that was already inhabited and shows traces of human activities. It reacts to the latter, for instance by using brick, the locally traditional building material, or by continuing or breaking up the row in which the house is situated. In the Müngersdorf neighbourhood, one often comes across curving walls around individual properties. These features too are adopted by Ungers: he transforms the junction of the little side street and Belvederestraße into a semicircular curve. He even uses this curve in the ground plan of the house. It reap-

bereits bewohnt war, Spuren menschlicher Tätigkeiten trägt. Auf sie reagiert es, beispielsweise im Aufgreifen des ortsüblichen Baumaterials Backstein oder in der Fortführung und Auflösung der Zeile, in der das Haus steht. Im Wohnquartier Müngersdorf trifft man mehrfach auf gerundete Grundstücksmauern. Auch sie greift Ungers auf, indem er die Einmündung der kleinen Nebenstraße in die Belvederestraße zu einer Halbkreiskurve umformt. Diese Rundung übernimmt er sogar in den Grundriß des Hauses. Sie kehrt wieder im Dreiviertelkreis der Besprechungsnische, auf die sich ihrerseits der Vollkreis des zentralen Treppenturms bezieht. Wenn Ungers der Ortsgeschichte Themen entnimmt, so sind die Variationen ganz und gar seine Komposition. Dem ursprünglichen Motiv gleichen sie so wenig oder so viel wie die Brahms-Variationen dem Thema von Haydn.

Das Verfahren der Variation, der Metamorphose und Transposition eines Motivs, das Ungers in seinen späteren Schriften oft angeführt und in seinem Werk ebenso oft angewendet hat, ist im Manifest nicht eigens erwähnt. Formation und Transformation waren für ihn jedoch zusammengehörende Prozesse. Sie »bedingen sich gegenseitig wie das Ein- und Ausatmen, wie Tag und Nacht. Formation ist nicht denkbar ohne Transformation, und umgekehrt gibt es keine Transformation, die nicht wieder eine andere Transformation hervorbringt.«[31]

Den Besuchern seines Hauses pflegte der Architekt die Entstehung dieser Variationsketten an der Abfolge der Stockwerke klarzumachen.[32] Unten verschließt sich das Haus, indem die Arbeits- und Wohnräume des Parterres von den stabilen Backsteinmauern um das Haus und seine Gärten abgedichtet werden. Licht und Grün (das im Schatten des Hauses nicht eben üppig gedeiht) sind zugelassen, nicht aber der Blick ins Freie und umgekehrt der Blick ins Innere. Die Schutzfunktion, »Bergung und Einhüllung« überwiegen. Nach oben zu lichtet sich die Baumasse auf, der Bau durchläuft Stufen der Befreiung. Die Fenster gewinnen größere Formate, der Blick reicht in die Nachbarschaft, die in Ausschnitten zugelassen wird. Öffnung und Transparenz nehmen zu. Im zweiten Obergeschoß gibt es Dachgarten, Balkon und den Überblick über die örtliche Situation. Der Himmel tut sich auf.

Das Wort von der Metamorphose erinnert an Johann Wolfgang Goethes *Metamorphose der Pflanzen*.[33] Ungers berief sich auf die Goethe-Lektüre, die er schon in seiner Studienzeit zur Kenntnis genommen haben will. »In dieser kleinen Schrift erschloß sich mir eine Ideenwelt, die sich nicht auf das Prinzip der Kausalität bezog, sondern auf die Umwandlung der Dinge durch die Metamorphose, nach welcher ein Teil den nächsten hervorbringt und die verschiedenen Gestalten durch Modifikation eines Grundprinzips entstehen«, erläuterte Ungers seinen Hörern bei passender Gelegenheit, als er nämlich 2002 die Goethe-Plakette der Stadt Frankfurt am Main empfing.[34] Über Goethes Morphologie hätte er sich im übrigen auch mit seinem Müngersdorfer Mitbürger Rudolf Schwarz unterhalten können, mit dem er sich in vielem einig wußte. Ungers bekannte sich posthum als »großer Verehrer von Schwarz«.[35]

Kritiker und Gesinnungsgenossen

Das Haus Ungers I war nicht das einzige, das aus der zeitgenössischen Hausproduktion hervorstach. In der Bundesrepublik bauten Wilfried Beck-Erlang, H. Peter Buddeberg, Heinz Mohl in den 1960er Jahren Einfamilienhäuser, die sich durch individuelle Formensprache, skulpturale Gestaltung der Volumen, taktiles Baumaterial, gewichtigen Auftritt und private Abgeschlossenheit von den offenen Bungalows der Moderne-Tradition unterschieden. Carlfried Mutschler errichtete 1960 in Mannheim ein eigenes Wohnhaus in hellem Ziegelstein und Beton, das eine Baulücke füllte und insofern auch Ungers' »Verantwortung gegenüber dem Ort« übernahm.

Im Karlsruher Raum entwarf Gesinnungsfreund Gieselmann Einfamilien- und Reihenhäuser, in denen er mehr oder weniger den Forderungen aus dem Manifest *Zu einer neuen Architektur* nachkam. Auch ein eigenes Haus entstand 1960–65. Im Raumprogramm ist es ähnlich vielseitig wie das Haus Ungers, im Erscheinungsbild gleichfalls reich differenziert und plastisch in der Auffassung. Es besitzt einen dreigeschossigen Wohnbereich des Bauherrn, Studio und Einliegerwohnungen in drei Baukörpern, die sich an einem steilen Hang um einen kleinen Patio gruppieren. Die Seitenansichten sind reich gestaffelt, wie eine architektonische Paraphrase des Hangs, der früher als Weinberg gedient hatte.

Gieselmann war 1953 mit der Vespa durch Skandinavien gekurvt. Der wichtigste Ertrag seiner Reise war die Bekanntschaft mit Alvar Aalto, ein »Schlüsselerlebnis«. Der große finnische Architekt erlaubte es ihm, in seinem Sommerhaus auf der Insel Muuratsalo zu übernachten. Aaltos Naturverständnis, sein Materialgefühl, sein Umgang mit Tages- und Kunstlicht, seine Einbeziehung von Kunst und künstlerischem Gerät hinterließen einen tiefen Eindruck, den Gieselmann auch seinem Freund Ungers übermittelte. »Es war für uns eine ganz neue Art Moderne – weder nach den uns geläufigen asketischen noch auch nach den ästhetischen Regeln konzipiert, sondern frei, gefühlvoll, sinnlich, asymmetrisch, gekurvt, im Spiel mit dem Licht, in der Einbeziehung der Natur.«[36] Aalto blieb über viele Jahre ein Stern auch an Ungers' Firmament, obwohl sich die konkreten Einflüsse in Grenzen hielten.

Kein Einfamilienhaus dürfte in Nachkriegsdeutschland und darüber hinaus so viel Aufsehen erregt haben wie das Haus Ungers in der Belvederestraße. Daran war zum Teil die Presse schuld, zum Teil waren es die internationalen Beziehungen, die Ungers schon zu dieser Zeit geknüpft hatte. Die erste Veröffentlichung erschien 1960 in der wöchentlichen Architekturzeitschrift *Bauwelt*, deren Chefredakteur Ulrich Conrads den jungen Architekten anfangs förderte, wo er konnte. In Heft 8, das Ungers gewidmet war, stand ein Photo des Hauses auf der Titelseite.[37]

Auch internationaler Besuch stellte sich in der Belvederestraße ein. Im Frühjahr 1960 – das Ungers-Heft der *Bauwelt* konnte eben erst erschienen sein – besuchten Aldo Rossi, Giorgio Grassi und Vittorio Gregotti im Auftrag der italienischen, international respektierten Architekturzeitschrift *Casabella* den *amico* Ungers. Der Artikel kam im Oktober heraus.[38] Ungers hatte seinen Gesprächspartnern offenbar ausführlich seine Gedanken über die Notwendigkeit erläutert, sich an der Realität des Ortes zu orientieren. Er verteidigte Vielfalt, Individualität, die Koexistenz vieler Meinungen und wehrte sich gegen Schlagworte. Den Schlagworten entging er allerdings nicht. Denn sein Domizil in der Belvederestraße avancierte zu einer Stilikone des so genannten Brutalismus, was andererseits den Vorteil hatte, ihm zu internationaler Bekanntheit zu verhelfen.

12. Oswald Mathias Ungers, Haus Belvederestraße 60, Köln-Müngersdorf, 1958/59. Zustand 1960. (Photo: Walter Ehmann.)
13. Carlfried Mutschler, Wohn- und Bürohaus Mutschler, Mannheim, E 7/7, 1960. (Photo: Joachim Langner.)
14. Reinhard Gieselmann, Wohn- und Atelierhaus Gieselmann, Karlsruhe-Durlach, Rittnertstraße 81, 1960 to 1965. (Photo: Sigrid Neubert.)

12. Oswald Mathias Ungers, Haus Belvederestraße 60, Müngersdorf, Cologne, 1958/59. State around 1960. (Photo: Walter Ehmann.)
13. Carlfried Mutschler, Mutschler residential and office building, Mannheim, E 7/7, 1960. (Photo: Joachim Langner.)
14. Reinhard Gieselmann, Gieselmann residential building and studio, Durlach, Karlsruhe, Rittnertstraße 81, 1960–65. (Photo: Sigrid Neubert.)

pears in the three-quarter circle of the conference niche, to which in turn the full circle of the central stairwell tower is a reference. When Ungers borrows themes from local history, the variations are very much his own composition. They have as little or as much resemblance to the original motif as do the Brahms variations to the theme by Haydn.

The method of variation, metamorphosis and transposition of a motif, which Ungers often referred to in his later writings and used in his work just as frequently, is not specifically mentioned in the manifesto. However, formation and transformation were for him processes that belonged together. They »are interdependent like breathing in and out, like day and night. Formation is not conceivable without transformation, and conversely there is no transformation that does not in turn produce another transformation.«[31]

To visitors of his house, the architect used to explain the origin of these chains of variations, using the succession of the floors as an example.[32] Below, the house shuts down: the workrooms and living rooms of the ground floor are insulated by the stable brick walls around the house and its gardens. Light and greenery (which hardly thrives in the shadow of the house) are allowed, but not a view of the outdoors and conversely a view of the indoors. The protective function, »to shelter and envelop«, predominates. Higher up the building becomes brighter, goes through stages of liberation. The windows now have larger formats, the view extends into the neighbourhood, which is visible in sections. Opening and transparency increase. On the second floor there is a roof garden, balcony and the view of the local situation. The sky unfolds.

The quotation about metamorphosis is reminiscent of Johann Wolfgang Goethe's *Metamorphose der Pflanzen* (Metamorphosis of plants).[33] Ungers was referring to his reading of Goethe, claiming he took note of the essay even as a student. »What was revealed to me in this short piece was a world of ideas that did not refer to the principle of causality but to the transformation of things through metamorphosis, according to which one part gives rise to the next and the various forms come about through the modification of a basic principle«, Ungers explained to his listeners when the opportunity arose, namely when, in 2002, he was awarded the Goethe-Plakette of the city of Frankfurt am Main.[34] Incidentally, it is also possible that he discussed Goethe's morphology with a fellow Müngersdorfer, the architect Rudolf Schwarz, with whom he agreed on many points. Ungers posthumously declared himself to be a »great admirer of Schwarz«.[35]

Critics and like-minded colleagues

The Ungers House I was not the only one to stand out among those built by his contemporaries. In the German Federal Republic, Wilfried Beck-Erlang, H. Peter Buddeberg, Heinz Mohl built single-family houses in the 1960s that differed from the open bungalows of the Modernist tradition due to their individual stylistic idiom, the sculptural design of the buildings, tactile building material, imposing appearance and private seclusion. In 1960 Carlfried Mutschler built his own residence in Mannheim of light-coloured brick and concrete that filled a gap site and in this respect also adhered to Ungers' »responsibility to the place«.

In the Karlsruhe area Ungers' like-minded friend Gieselmann designed single-family and row houses in which he more or less fulfilled the demands of the manifesto *Zu einer neuen Architektur*. He, too, designed his own house in 1960–65. Spatially it is just as multifaceted as the Ungers house, and its appearance is just as richly differentiated und three-dimensionally conceived. It has a three-storey living area for the owner, a studio and flats for lodgers in buildings grouped on a steep slope around a small patio. The side elevations are intensely staggered, like an architectonic paraphrase of the slope, which was formerly a vineyard.

In 1953 Gieselmann took his Vespa on a tour of Scandinavia. The most important result of his journey was his meeting with Alvar Aalto, a »key experience«. The great Finnish architect allowed him to spend the night at his summerhouse on the island of Muuratsalo. Aalto's understanding of nature, his feeling for materiality, the way he handled daylight and artificial light, the way he included art and artistic furnishings left a deep impression, which Gieselmann also communicated to his friend Ungers. »We felt it was a completely new type of Modernism – conceived neither according to the ascetic rules familiar to us nor according to aesthetic rules, but free, expressive, sensuous, asymmetrical, curved, in interplay with light, integrating the natural world.«[36] For many years Aalto continued to be a star in Ungers' firmament as well, although his concrete influence was limited.

No single-family home probably caused as big a stir in postwar Germany and beyond as did the Ungers House in Belvederestraße. It was partly the press that was to blame, and partly the international contacts Ungers had already established by then. The first public reference to the building appeared in 1960 in the architecture weekly *Bauwelt*, whose editor in chief, Ulrich Conrads, initially promoted the young architect wherever he could. The title page of issue no. 8, dedicated to Ungers, showed a photo of the house.[37]

International visitors also appeared in Belvederestraße. In the spring of 1960 – the Ungers issue of *Bauwelt* had probably just been published – Aldo Rossi, Giorgio Grassi and Vittorio Gregotti visited their *amico* Ungers on the instructions of the internationally respected Italian architecture journal *Casabella*. The article was published in October.[38] Ungers had obviously given his interviewers a detailed explanation of his ideas about the need to be guided by the reality of a place. He defended variety, individuality and the coexistence of many views, and protested against slogans. He could not avoid slogans, however. For his residence in Belvederestraße became a style icon of the so-called Brutalist movement, which on the other hand had the advantage of helping him gain international recognition.

He owed this promotion to the British architecture critic and historian Reyner Banham, who in 1966 included the house in his book *The New Brutalism*. Banham was one of those historians who devote a considerable part of their time and energy to the definition of styles. His attempt to explain the slogan Brutalism or – since it is originally an English term and was uttered with faint irony – *New Brutalism*, ranges from descriptions of precise steel buildings in emulation of Mies van der Rohe[39] to »brick Brutalists« – as he referred to them – and concrete sculptors such as Walter Förderer or Vittoriano Viganò. The works of his Brutalists look so different from each other that Banham had to resort to intellectual cat-

Diese Beförderung war dem englischen Architekturkritiker und -historiker Reyner Banham zu verdanken, der das Haus 1966 in sein Buch *Brutalismus* aufnahm. Banham gehörte zu den Historikern, die einen beträchtlichen Teil ihrer Zeit und Arbeitskraft der Definition von Stilen widmen. Sein Versuch, das Schlagwort Brutalismus oder – da es aus dem englischen Sprachraum stammt und mit leichter Ironie vorgetragen wurde – *New Brutalism* zu erläutern, reicht von präzisen Stahlbauten in der Nachfolge Mies van der Rohes[39] bis zu den von ihm so genannten »Backsteinbrutalisten« und Betonskulpteuren wie Walter Förderer oder Vittoriano Viganò. Das Erscheinungsbild seiner Brutalisten ist so unterschiedlich, daß Banham intellektuelle Kategorien zur Begriffsbestimmung heranziehen mußte: Bildhaftigkeit, Ablesbarkeit und Betonung der Konstruktion, »brutale« Ehrlichkeit in der Verwendung der Materialien, Berücksichtigung von Situationen und Baustoffen »as found«, Masse und Plastizität.

Ungers' Haus sei »vielleicht das einzige qualitätvolle Bauwerk in Nordeuropa, das mit dem Werk der Vertreter der Neoliberty in Italien verglichen werden kann«, meinte Banham. Mit »Neoliberty« war eine von *Casabella* unterstützte Stilrichtung gemeint, die sich in Erinnerung an den Liberty-Stil, den italienischen Jugendstil, neben Rationalismus und *architettura organica* etablierte. Der Vergleich falle aber zugunsten von Ungers aus, wegen dessen historischer Bildung und seiner Fähigkeit, Bildungseindrücke zu verarbeiten. Banham dachte an Erich Mendelsohn oder Hugo Häring. Was die Lage des Hauses am Abschluß einer Häuserzeile betraf, fühlte er sich an Gerrit Thomas Rietvelds Haus Schröder in Utrecht (1923–25) erinnert, das als ein Hauptwerk der holländischen De Stijl-Bewegung gilt.[40]

Rietveld hatte allerdings auf den scharfen Kontrast des Modernen gegen das überlieferte Alte gesetzt. Seine leichte Komposition aus Linien und Flächen ist wie eine Botschaft aus einer anderen Welt an die Brandmauer der älteren und höheren Zeile geheftet. Ungers dagegen führte Vorgaben wie das Sichtmauerwerk und die Farbigkeit der Nachbarbebauung weiter, zum Teil auch Gebäudehöhe, Dachfirst und Traufe. Er nahm sich nie gesehene Freiheiten, ließ aber trotzdem die eigene Formenwahl aus den lokalen Gegebenheiten hervorgehen.

Mit diesen Publikationen wurde das Müngersdorfer Haus zu einer Zielscheibe der Kritik.[41] Prominente Kritiker nahmen es als Beispiel für eine Entwicklung, die bewährte Prinzipien und Methoden der Moderne zu verraten schien. Willkür und Neues um jeden Preis drohten. Sigfried Giedion, ein Doyen der Architekturkritik, entdeckte überall »Playboy-Architektur«: »Die Architektur wird behandelt, wie ein Playboy das Leben behandelt – schnell aller Dinge überdrüssig und von einer Sensation zur anderen hastend.«[42] In der Schweizer Zeitschrift *Bauen und Wohnen* forderten Jürgen Joedicke, Autor einer *Geschichte der modernen Architektur* (1958), und der Architekt Franz Füeg »geistige Zucht« und bildeten eine Seite mit neun Bauten ab, die ihnen offenbar als Exempel der Zuchtlosigkeit erschienen. Neben Gottfried Böhm war auch Ungers mit der Belvederestraße vertreten.[43] Gieselmann und Ungers verteidigten sich ihrerseits, traten für das Wagnis der Kunst ein, für die geistige Freiheit, gegen Erstarrung und Schematisierung.

Eine der in Deutschland seltenen Debatten über Architektur begann, und das unschuldige Müngersdorfer Haus war einer ihrer Auslöser. Da die Diskussion und der Name ihres Protagonisten dank Banham und den drei *Casabella*-Redakteuren ins Ausland gedrungen waren, regten Bauten von Ungers auch dort zur Kritik an. Sir Nikolaus Pevsner konstatierte beunruhigt eine »Wiederkehr des Historismus« und nicht zuletzt des Expressionismus. Die Verwendung »ineinander verschachtelter Blöcke«, wie sie Mies van der Rohe bei seinem Berliner Denkmal für Rosa Luxemburg und Karl Liebknecht (1926) benutzt hatte, fand er bei Ungers wieder. Das Müngersdorfer Haus bildete er daher auch in seinem Sündenkatalog von 1961 zusammen mit rund dreißig anderen Übeltätern ab.[44]

Ungers konnte sich von dem Vergleich nicht unangenehm berührt fühlen, weil er selbst begonnen hatte, sich mit der Expressionistengruppe um Paul Scheerbart und Bruno Taut aus der Zeit unmittelbar nach dem Ersten Weltkrieg zu beschäftigen.[45] Er kaufte eine Sammlung expressionistischer Zeichnungen zusammen, veranstaltete 1963 gemeinsam mit dem Leverkusener Museumsleiter Udo Kultermann die Ausstellung »Die gläserne Kette«, die von Schloß Morsbroich in die Berliner Akademie der Künste wanderte, und gab die Briefe der in Deutschland verstreut lebenden, hauptsächlich aber Berliner Künstler und Architekten der Revolutionsjahre nach 1918 heraus.[46] Tenor dieser Aktivitäten aus Expressionistentagen war revolutionärer Künstlerwille. Eine solche Entdeckung früher Gesinnungsgenossen mußte Ungers zum Zeitpunkt der Attacken auf seinen Hausbau gelegen kommen, denn: »Bauen ist etwas anderes als Mauern – Bauen ist Ausdruck einer geistigen Weltvorstellung.«[47] Darin war er mit den Expressionisten einig.

Aber schon im Laufe der frühen 1960er Jahre wandte Ungers sich von allzu heftig-utopischen Bekundungen ab. Sein gesammeltes Material zum deutschen Expressionismus stellte er anderen Autoren wie den italienischen Historikern Franco Borsi und Giovanni Klaus König zur Verfügung*, con una franca amicizia e aperta cameraderie*. Es wirkte wie ein Abschied von diesem Thema. Borsi und König machten aus den *segreti della biblioteca della sua bellissima casa* ein umfangreiches Buch, das eine Zeitlang die maßgebliche Darstellung des Expressionismus in der Architektur blieb.[48]

Ungers selbst referierte auf einem internationalen Kongreß über die Kunstformen des Expressionismus, der 1964 in Florenz stattfand, bereits ziemlich leidenschaftslos über »die Erscheinungsformen des Expressionismus in der Architektur«.[49] Er fragte sich – wie auch Sigfried Giedion[50] –, ob man den Begriff Expressionismus überhaupt auf die Architektur übertragen könne. Expressionistische Erscheinungsformen könnten sich lediglich auf mehr oder weniger visionäre und utopische Bauprojekte beschränken. »Dies liegt in der Architektur selbst begründet, die ihrem Wesen nach in weit größerem Maße als die übrigen Künste an den Stoff, den Zweck, die Konstruktion und die Aufgabe gebunden ist.«[51] Anders als im Gieselmann-Ungers-Manifest gestand Ungers dem Bauwerk nun zu, rationalen Überlegungen und nicht nur irrationalen Impulsen zu folgen, den Funktionen wie den Inspirationen. Der Weg war frei zu neuen Positionen. Mit der früheren teilten sie jedoch den Anspruch auf das souveräne Recht des Künstlers auf seine künstlerisch-intellektuellen Entscheidungen.

Mit dem Hause leben

Eine besondere Eigenschaft des Müngersdorfer Hauses stellte sich im jahrzehntelangen Gebrauch heraus: seine Veränderbarkeit. Ein derart festes, ausdrucksstarkes Ge-

15. Gerrit Thomas Rietveld, Haus Schröder, Utrecht, 1923–25. (Photo: Klaus Kinold.)
16. Ludwig Mies van der Rohe, Denkmal für Rosa Luxemburg und Karl Liebknecht, Berlin-Friedrichsfelde, 1926. (Photo: Mies van der Rohe Archive, Museum of Modern Art, New York.)

15. Gerrit Thomas Rietveld, Schröder house, Utrecht, 1923–25. (Photo: Klaus Kinold.)
16. Ludwig Mies van der Rohe, memorial for Rosa Luxemburg and Karl Liebknecht, Friedrichsfelde, Berlin, 1926. (Photo: Mies van der Rohe Archive, Museum of Modern Art, New York.)

egories in order to define the term: a pictorial, readable and emphatic structure, »brutally« honest use of materials, with locations and building materials taken into account »as found«, mass and plasticity.

Ungers' house, wrote Banham, was »perhaps the only high-quality building in Northern Europe that can be compared with the work of representatives of the Neoliberty movement in Italy«. By »Neoliberty« he meant a style promoted by *Casabella* which recalled the Liberty style, or Italian Art Nouveau, and which established itself alongside rationalism and *architettura organica*. But the comparison, according to Banham, favoured Ungers, because of the latter's historical education and his ability to process all that he had learned. Banham had Erich Mendelsohn or Hugo Häring in mind. As far as the location of the house at the end of a row of houses was concerned, he was reminded of Gerrit Thomas Rietveld's Schröder House in Utrecht (1923–25), considered to be a principal work of the Dutch De Stijl movement.[40]

Rietveld, however, had focused on the sharp contrast of the Modernist style as opposed to age-old tradition. His light composition of lines and surfaces is like a message from another world posted on the firewall of the older and taller row of houses. Ungers, on the other hand, continued to use such features as exposed masonry and the colour scheme of adjacent architecture, and in part the height of buildings, roof ridge and eaves. He took unprecedented liberties, yet made sure his own choice of forms evolved from local conditions.

As a result of the above-named publications, the Müngersdorf house became a target for criticism.[41] Prominent critics considered it to be an example of a development that seemed to betray the tried and tested principles and methods of Modernism. They feared the impending threat of arbitrariness and of novelty at any price. Sigfried Giedion, a dean of architectural criticism, discovered »playboy architecture« everywhere: »They treat architecture the way a playboy treats life – quickly tired of everything and rushing from one sensation to the next.«[42] In the Swiss journal *Bauen und Wohnen* Jürgen Joedicke, the author of a *Geschichte der modernen Architektur* (History of modern architecture) (1958), and the architect Franz Füeg called for »intellectual discipline«, adding a page of illustrations that showed nine buildings they apparently considered to be examples of lack of discipline. In addition to Gottfried Böhm, Ungers and his Belvederestraße building were also represented.[43] In turn, Gieselmann und Ungers defended themselves, advocating art as an act of daring, calling for intellectual freedom, and protesting against rigidity and schematisation.

This marked the beginning of a debate about architecture, a rare occurrence in Germany, and the innocent Müngersdorf house was one of the things that triggered it. Since, thanks to Banham and the three editors of *Casabella*, the discussion and the name of its protagonist had become public knowledge abroad, the buildings of Ungers aroused criticism there as well. Sir Nikolaus Pevsner was alarmed to note a »return to Historicism« and, not least, Expressionism. In the work of Ungers he again discovered the use of »blocks nested inside one another«, of a type used by Mies van der Rohe in his Berlin memorial for Rosa Luxemburg and Karl Liebknecht (1926). That was why he included a picture of the Müngersdorf house in his 1961 list of transgressions together with some thirty other wrongdoers.[44]

Ungers could not take exception to the comparison, because he himself had begun to devote his attention to the group of Expressionists around Paul Scheerbart and Bruno Taut, from the period immediately after World War I.[45] He purchased a collection of Expressionist drawings; in 1963, together with the Leverkusen museum director Udo Kultermann, he organised the exhibition »The Glass Chain«, which later moved from Morsbroich Castle to the Berlin Akademie der Künste, and published the letters of artists and architects of the years of revolution after 1918, who lived dispersed in Germany but mainly in Berlin.[46] The tenor of these activities from Expressionist days was revolutionary artistic intention. Ungers' discovery of others who shared his views must have come at an opportune time, just as his new house was coming under attack, for: »Building is something more than walls – building is the expression of a spiritual view of the world.«[47] On this he and the Expressionists were in agreement.

Already in the early 1960s, however, Ungers turned away from overly vehement utopian proclamations. He made his collected material on German Expressionism available to other authors, such as the Italian historians Franco Borsi and Giovanni Klaus König, *con una franca amicizia e aperta cameraderie*. It felt like a leave-taking from this topic. Borsi and König made a sizable book out of the *segreti della biblioteca della sua bellissima casa*, which for awhile was the authoritative volume on Expressionism in architecture.[48]

Ungers himself lectured, somewhat dispassionately by this time, on »manifestations of Expressionism in architecture« at an international congress on the art forms of Expressionism held in Florence in 1964.[49] He wondered – as did Sigfried Giedion[50] – whether it was even possible to apply the term Expressionism to architecture. Expressionist manifestations, he felt, could be limited only to more or less visionary and utopian construction projects. »This is due to the nature of architecture itself, which is subject to material, purpose, construction and design to a far greater extent than the other arts.«[51] Unlike in the Gieselmann-Ungers manifesto, Ungers now conceded that a building follows rational considerations and not only irrational impulses – functions as well as inspirations. The way was open to new perspectives. These did have something in common with the former ones, however: the claim that the artist has a sovereign right to his artistic and intellectual decisions.

Living with the house

One particular quality of the Müngersdorf house became apparent over decades of use: its changeability. One would have thought such a solid, expressive structure would baulk at any transformation. But the opposite turned out to be the case. The house showed itself to be amazingly willing to change. When, after Ungers' stays in America, the architectural office was again enlarged, partition walls were removed. The garage and garage driveway on Belvederestraße were eliminated. The lower granny flat was used to house studio drafting tables, while the upper one was incorporated in the private zone as a library. Brick walls were plastered in white. Definite form and alterable function do not have to be irreconcilable contradictions. The flexibility of this house lay in the adaptability of a defined form, not the instant variability of a serviceable conversion system.

häuse, sollte man meinen, sperrt sich gegen jede Umwandlung. Aber das Gegenteil war der Fall. Das Haus legte eine erstaunliche Veränderungsbereitschaft an den Tag. Als sich das Architekturbüro nach den Amerika-Aufenthalten des Hausherrn wieder vergrößerte, wurden Zwischenwände herausgenommen. Garage und Garageneinfahrt an der Belvederestraße fielen weg. Die untere Einliegerwohnung nahm Zeichentische des Ateliers auf, die obere wurde als Bibliothek der privaten Zone zugeschlagen. Backsteinwände wurden weiß geputzt. Bestimmte Form und wandelbarer Zweck müssen keine unvereinbaren Widersprüche sein. Die Flexibilität dieses Hauses war die Wandlungsfähigkeit einer definierten Gestalt, nicht die hurtige Variabilität eines funktionstüchtigen Umbausystems. Sogar eine Kassettendecke, die ausgerechnet der Ehrlichkeitsfanatiker Ungers sich gewünscht hatte, wurde in einem Raum der ehemaligen oberen Einliegerwohnung nachträglich und vorübergehend eingezogen.

Sogar der Auftritt des Hauses hat sich verändert. Das vormals leere Nachbargrundstück gegenüber an der Nebenstraße ist verbaut, dem Ungers-Haus damit ein Stück provokanter Isolation genommen. Die Bäume sind gewachsen und haben den Bau kleiner werden lassen. Die Fülle der Bauformen ist geblieben, aber nach den auftrumpfenden Gewalttaten anderer scheint sie sich beruhigt zu haben. Heute wirkt sie fast zierlich, kleinteilig, nicht brutal, sondern im Gegenteil spielerisch, handwerklich gediegen im Ganzen wie im Einzelnen. Im sorgfältigen Mauerverband sitzen Betonbänder und Wasserspeier wie Schmuckstücke. Die größte Veränderung, ob wohl nicht auf den ersten Blick wahrnehmbar, entstand durch die Doppelfenster, die in den 1980er Jahren eingesetzt wurden. Die äußeren Scheiben sitzen bündig in den Außenflächen und egalisieren die zuvor tief schattenden Fassaden.

Bildende Kunst war für Ungers nicht eine Liebhaberei, sondern eine notwendige Orientierungshilfe, Teil seines Kosmos, zu dem das Bauen, die architekturwissenschaftliche Lektüre, Skulptur, Malerei und Photographie gehörten. Er hat nicht alles gesammelt, aber vieles, was ihn und seine Arbeit berührte. Sein Interesse setzte schon bei der Antike ein. Ungers besaß griechische und römische Skulpturen und Kapitelle und Abgüsse davon, Darstellungen antiker Bauten in Gemälden Leo von Klenzes oder Turpin de Crissés, historische Modelle in Holz oder Kork. Den Modellbauer und Künstler Bernd Grimm ließ er jahrelang Ikonen der Baugeschichte wie den Parthenon in Athen, das Pantheon in Rom, das apulische Castel del Monte oder den Tempietto Donato Bramantes in Rom, der seinerzeit sogar von Zeitgenossen für ein antik-römisches Bauwerk gehalten wurde, maßstabsgetreu in Gipsmodellen nachbauen.[52]

Auch der Architektur der französischen Revolution, des Klassizismus und der Romantik mit ihren Architekturvisionen galt sein Interesse, dann aber intensiv und extensiv den Avantgarden des 20. Jahrhunderts. Welcher private Sammler mit historisch so weit ausgreifenden Themen konnte sich gleichzeitig eines Piet Mondrian und eines Gerhard Richter, eines Ellsworth Kelly und eines Dan Flavin rühmen! Mancher Ankauf erklärt sich aus Ungers' späterer Faszination durch das Quadrat, dessen Bearbeitungsformen bei anderen Künstlern er nachging: so bei Josef Albers, Carl Andre, Sol LeWitt, Gerhard Merz oder Bruce Nauman. Anderes war durch das Berufsinteresse des Architekten berührt, wie die aus Neonröhren zusammengestellte Lichtsäule Dan Flavins oder das »Dachpfannen«-Bild des Düsseldorfer Akademiekollegen Markus Lüpertz.

Kunst sorgte im Haus an der Belvederestraße durch sich selbst für Bewegung. Vieles wechselte seinen Platz, weil die Bauherren ihre Prioritäten änderten, weil Ankäufe hinzukamen und andere Nachbarschaften erforderten, weil Kunstwerke für Ausstellungen ausgeliehen waren und monate- oder jahrelang nicht zurückkehrten. Der einzige größere Hof, der nach dem Bau der Bibliothek unbebaut blieb, wirkte jeweils anders, je nachdem ob dort die sechs toskanischen, im Kunsthandel ersteigerten Säulen standen und einen Peristylhof darstellten oder/und die Stahlprofile des *Square* von Bruce Nauman oder/und die Felsbrocken des *Basalt Circle* von Richard Long ausgelegt waren. Fast zu erwarten, daß Ungers auch eine Ikone des deutschen Klassizismus variierte, den *Stein des guten Glücks*, den Goethe 1777 in seinem Weimarer Garten aufstellen ließ: Kugel auf Quader. Ungers ließ ihn von Hubert Becker ausarbeiten.

Seit seinen Projekten für Düsseldorf und Köln (1960) hat Ungers, inzwischen von der Fachwelt gern OMU abgekürzt, mehrere Museen entworfen und seit dem Deutschen Architekturmuseum in Frankfurt am Main (1979–84) auch gebaut. Sein eigenes Haus zeigt nicht die Disposition eines wenn auch kleinen Museums. Bilder und Skulpturen wurden anfangs dorthin gehängt und gestellt, wo Platz war – anders als bei seinen großen Bauaufträgen, wo ihm die Zusammenarbeit mit Künstlern von Anfang an wichtig war. In räumlicher Disposition und Lichtführung nahm die Architektur erst mit dem Bibliothekskubus Rücksicht auf dort zu plazierende Kunstwerke.

Nach dem postumen Verkauf des Hauses am Kämpchensweg und dem erneuten Umzug von Büchern zurück in die Belvederestraße wirkt das »alte« Haus in manchen Räumen sogar überfüllt. Denn deren Proportionen waren bei aller Vielfalt des Komplexes Proportionen der späten fünfziger Jahre – relativ kleine, relativ niedrige Zimmer ohne repräsentative hohe oder zweigeschossige Räume, wie sie heute in den Luxusvillen der Bauzeitschriften die Regel sind. Möbliert war das Haus entweder mit gediegenen Stilmöbeln oder den modularen Holzmöbeln, die Ungers seit den 1950er Jahren selbst entwarf (System Kubus, System Kreis, rechtwinklige Gerüstentwürfe für das Deutsche Architekturmuseum) und von Schreinern herstellen ließ. Die Bequemlichkeit des Sitzenden war dabei kein Entwurfsparameter, wohl aber waren es die Maße und Proportionen der Architektur. Den Stuhl Leonardo von 1991 entwarf er nach den Vorgaben der vitruvianischen Proportionsfigur.

Ein Kubus für Bücher

Die größte Veränderung, die der Baugruppe widerfuhr, war der Bau der Bibliothek auf einem Teil des Grundstücks, wo bisher einer der ummauerten Gärten gewesen war. Die Seitenstraße der Belvederestraße heißt hier zufälligerweise Quadrather Straße. Der Name erklärt sich aus einem nicht allzu weit entfernten Ort westlich von Köln namens Quadrath, paßt aber hervorragend zu jener geometrischen Figur, die im Spätwerk von Ungers einen Vorzugsplatz erhielt, das Quadrat. Quadratisch ist der Grundriß der Bibliothek, quadratisch der Schnitt des Bücherturms, der zu einem Drittel, nämlich mit seinem Kellergeschoß, in die Erde versenkt ist. Quadratisch sind die Luken im Steinmantel des Gebäudes, kubisch die

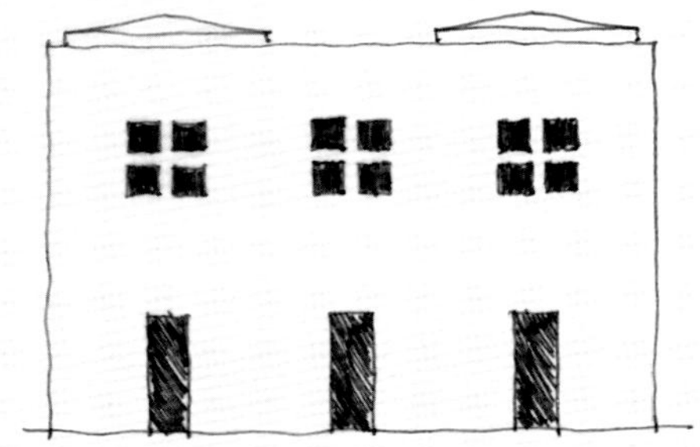

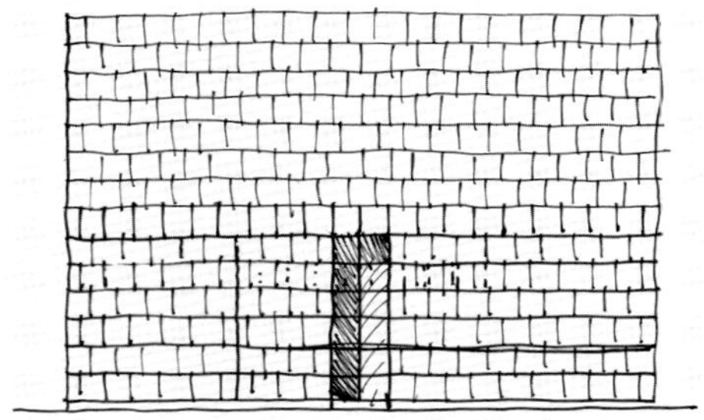

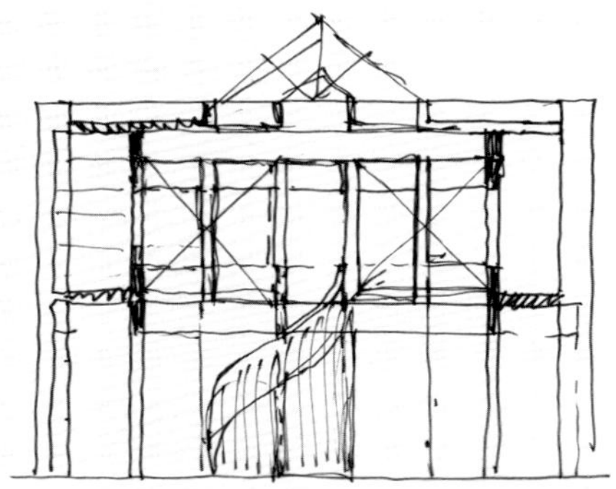

17–19. Oswald Mathias Ungers, Haus Belvederestraße 60, Köln-Müngersdorf. Bibliothek, 1989/90. Skizzen von Oswald Mathias Ungers.
20. Oswald Mathias Ungers, Haus Belvederestraße 60, Köln-Müngersdorf. Bibliothek. Arbeitsmodell. (Photo: Dieter Leistner.)

17–19. Oswald Mathias Ungers, Haus Belvederestraße 60, Müngersdorf, Cologne. Library, 1989/90. Sketches by Oswald Mathias Ungers.
20. Oswald Mathias Ungers, Haus Belvederestraße 60, Müngersdorf, Cologne. Library. Working model. (Photo: Dieter Leistner.)

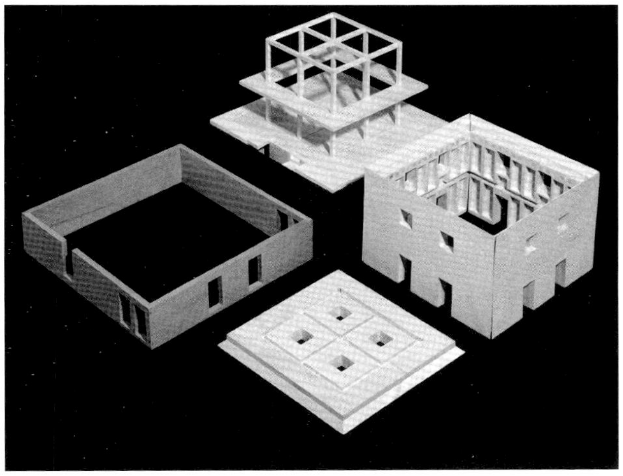

Even a coffered ceiling, which ironically Ungers, a fanatic for honesty, had wanted to have, was later and temporarily installed in a room of the former upper granny flat.

Even the outer view of the house has changed. The previously empty adjacent property opposite, on the side street, is now built up, thus depriving the Ungers House of some of its provocative isolation. The trees have grown and the building seems smaller. The design features are still as abundant as ever, but now, after the boastful acts of violence of other architects, this abundance seems less turbulent. Today it seems almost delicate, intricate, not brutal, but quite the contrary – playful, tastefully crafted both as a whole and in detail. In the careful wall bond, concrete bands and waterspouts are set like ornaments. The biggest change, although not obvious at first glance, came about as a result of the double windows that were installed in the 1980s. The panes of the storm windows are flush-mounted in the exterior surfaces and level the façades, which formerly used to cast deep shadows.

For Ungers the fine arts were not a hobby but something he needed in order to find his bearings, part of his cosmos, which included building, reading matter on the science of architecture, sculpture, painting and photography. He did not collect everything, but did collect many things that touched him and his work. His interest began already with antiquity. Ungers owned Greek and Roman sculptures and capitals and casts of them, representations of ancient Greek and Roman buildings in paintings by Leo von Klenze or Turpin de Crissé, historical models of wood or cork. For many years he commissioned the model builder and artist Bernd Grimm to build to scale plaster models of icons of architectural history, such as the Parthenon in Athens, the Pantheon in Rome, the Castel del Monte in Apulia or Donato Bramante's Tempietto in Rome, once taken for an ancient Roman building even by contemporaries.[52]

He was also interested in the architecture of the French Revolution, of classicism and romanticism with their architectural visions, and finally, intensively and extensively, in the avant-gardes of the 20th century. What private collector with such historically wide-ranging themes could boast that he owned both a Piet Mondrian and a Gerhard Richter, an Ellsworth Kelly and a Dan Flavin! Many a purchase can be explained by Ungers' later fascination with the square, whose treatment by other artists he studied: for instance, in the work of Josef Albers, Carl Andre, Sol LeWitt, Gerhard Merz or Bruce Nauman. Other purchases were motivated by an architect's professional interest, for instance Dan Flavin's light column, composed of neon tubes, or the picture »Roof Tiles« by Ungers' Düsseldorf academy colleague Markus Lüpertz.

In the Belvederestraße house, art itself ensured that there was movement. Many things changed places because the owners changed their priorities, because new purchases arrived and required different settings, because works of art had been lent to exhibitions and did not return for months and years. The only sizeable courtyard that had remained vacant after the construction of the library had a different effect every time, depending on whether the six Tuscan columns, bought at an art auction, stood in it representing a peristyle courtyard or/and the steel sections of Bruce Nauman's *Square* or/and the boulders of Richard Long's *Basalt Circle* were displayed there. It was almost predictable that Ungers put up the replica of an icon of German Classicism here – the *Stone of good fortune* Goethe had placed in his Weimar garden in 1777: a sphere on a cubic stone. Ungers commissioned Hubert Becker to make it for him.

Since his projects for Düsseldorf and Cologne (1960), Ungers – whose name in the meantime was abbreviated by his colleagues to OMU – designed several museums and, after the Deutsches Architekturmuseum in Frankfurt am Main (1979–84), built them as well. His own house does not have the disposition of even a small museum. Paintings and sculptures were initially hung and placed wherever there was room – unlike in his major construction projects, where collaboration with artists was important for him from the very start. As far as spatial disposition and lighting went, it was not until the library cube that Ungers' architectural designs took into account works of art that would be placed in a space.

After the posthumous sale of the house on Kämpchensweg, and once books had again been moved back to Belvederestraße, some of the rooms in the »old« house even felt crowded. For no matter how versatile the complex was, their proportions were the proportions of the late fifties – relatively small, relatively low rooms without representative high-ceilinged or two-storey rooms of a type today normally found in the luxury villas of the architectural journals. The house was furnished either with high-quality period furniture or modular wooden furniture that Ungers had been designing himself since the 1950s (Cube System, Circle System, rectangular frame designs for the Deutsches Architekturmuseum) and that he commissioned carpenters to make. The comfort of those who sat in the chairs was not one of the parameters of the design: rather, it was the measurements and proportions of the building. He designed the Leonardo chair, in 1991, based on the data of the Vitruvian Canon of Proportions.

A cube for books

The biggest change undergone by the complex of buildings was the construction of the library on part of the property where one of the walled gardens had previously been. The side street of Belvederestraße at this point is coincidentally called Quadrather Straße. The name is derived from a nearby village west of Cologne called Quadrath, but is remarkably appropriate in view of the geometrical figure Ungers favoured in his late work, the square (German: *Quadrat*). That is the shape of the ground plan of the library and of the section of the book tower, a third of which – the basement storey – is below the ground. It is the shape of the hatches in the building's stone envelope, while the four skylights installed on the roof are cubical. They are reminiscent of the white rods of the minimalist work of Sol Le Witt (1984) that was part of Ungers' collection.

In Ungers' work the square evolved into a form that creates order in the chaos of the world, a figure in which all differences and deviations are immobilised: equal length, equal height, equal width. It guarantees a very timeless look that »is touched by the breath of eternity. It attains permanence and stability, and saves one from the temptation to succumb to the trendy enticements of the prevailing spirit of the time, which is so short-lived that it would at once be followed by repentance for yesterday's enthusiasm« (Fritz Neumeyer).[53]

vier aufgesetzten Oberlichter auf dem Dach. Sie erinnern an das weiße Gestänge der minimalistischen Arbeit von Sol Le Witt (1984), das zum Kunstbesitz Ungers gehört.

Das Quadrat entwickelte sich bei Ungers zur Ordnungsform in den Wirren der Welt, zu jener Figur, in der alle Differenzen und Abweichungen stillgestellt sind: gleiche Länge, gleiche Höhe, gleiche Breite. Es garantiert eine möglichst zeitlose Erscheinung, die »einen Hauch von Ewigkeit gewinnt. Es gewinnt Permanenz und Stabilität und bewahrt vor der Versuchung, den modischen Verlockungen des jeweiligen Zeitgeists anheimzufallen, dessen Kurzatmigkeit die Reue über die Begeisterung von gestern auf dem Fuße folgen lassen würde« (Fritz Neumeyer).[53]

Den Photos der Innenräume nach zu urteilen, scheint der Bücherbestand des Ehepaars Ungers bis in die 1960er Jahre hinein nicht groß gewesen zu sein. Die Beschäftigung mit dem Expressionismus wird einen ersten Schub ausgelöst haben, die Berliner Vorlesungstätigkeit einen zweiten. Ungers' Neuorientierung hin zur Theorie weckte in ihm den Wunsch, die wichtigen Schriften der Architekturgeschichte selbst zu besitzen. So sind die Bibliomanen: Sie gehen nicht in die öffentliche Bibliothek, sondern kaufen sich lieber eine eigene zusammen. Lesen war für Ungers »eine schwere Arbeit, eine Anstrengung«.[54] Der Besitz der Bücher macht deren Studium jederzeit möglich, unabhängig von Öffnungszeiten und Leserkontrolle. Mehr noch: das kostbare Buch mit seinen Botschaften aus Jahrhunderten und Jahrtausenden strahlt für den empfänglichen Leser eine kultische Aura aus.

In den 1960er Jahren kaufte Ungers bei dem Bibliothekar und Antiquar Menno Hertzberger in Amsterdam ein,[55] der in seinem Fach eine Zelebrität war. Der Ankauf wurde zum Kern einer Büchersammlung von über 12 000 Bänden, die unter Architekturfreunden einen legendären Ruhm genießt. Unter den privaten Fachbibliotheken kann sich vermutlich nur die (allerdings umfangreichere) des Kunst- und Architekturhistorikers Werner Oechslin in Einsiedeln mit ihr messen.[56] Schwer vorstellbar übrigens, daß Ungers Vitruv und Alberti fließend auf Latein gelesen haben sollte. Mit Sicherheit konnte er die russischsprachige Literatur des sowjetischen Konstruktivismus, die er auch sammelte, nicht entziffern. Gläubige empfangen die segensreiche Wirkung von Reliquien ja auch nicht auf den Wegen des Verstandes.

Vom Bau seines ersten Hauses bis zum Bau seiner Bibliothek hatte OMU einen weiten Weg zurückgelegt. Nach seiner Rückkehr aus den USA ließen sich die Kontakte zu Auftraggebern in Deutschland zunächst zögerlich an. Eine Wende brachte der programmatische Bau des Deutschen Architekturmuseums in Frankfurt am Main (1979–84), den er dessen Direktor Heinrich Klotz verdankte, und der gleichzeitigen Badischen Landesbibliothek in Karlsruhe. Das Architekturmuseum war eine prestigehaltige Aufgabe, die eine Auseinandersetzung mit historischem Bestand verlangte, mit einer Doppelvilla aus der Zeit knapp vor dem Ersten Weltkrieg.[57] Vor allem bot der Auftrag für eine der Baukunst gewidmete Institution die Chance, sich mit Grundprinzipien des Bauens auseinanderzusetzen wie dem Motiv des Einhausens und der morphologischen Formenentwicklung.

Die Badische Landesbibliothek entstand gegenüber der Kirche St. Stephan des Karlsruher Baudirektors Friedrich Weinbrenner (1766–1826), von dessen klassizistischer Disziplin und Klarheit der Ungers-Entwurf profitierte. Zehn Jahre später ging Ungers daran, seiner eigenen Büchersammlung ein noch disziplinierteres und strengeres, allerdings auch unvergleichbar viel kleineres Gebäude zu verschaffen. Ungers hatte eine Leitvorstellung für

21. Oswald Mathias Ungers, Deutsches Architekturmuseum, Frankfurt am Main, 1979–84. (Photo: Stefan Müller.)

22. Oswald Mathias Ungers, Badische Landesbibliothek, Karlsruhe, 1980–92. (Photo: Dieter Leistner.)

Judging by the photos of the interior rooms, Ungers and his wife do not seem to have owned a large number of books until well into the 1960s. No doubt their preoccupation with Expressionism triggered the first impetus, while Ungers' work as a lecturer in Berlin triggered a second. Ungers' new approach to theory made him want to own the important writings of architectural history himself. That's what bibliomaniacs are like: They do not go to the public library, but prefer to purchase a library of their own. For Ungers, reading was »hard work, exertion«.[54] The fact that he owned the books made it possible for him to study them at any time, regardless of opening times and control of readers. What is more, for a receptive reader a precious book with its messages from past centuries and millennia emanates a ritualistic aura.

In the 1960s Ungers was a customer of the librarian and antiquarian bookseller Menno Hertzberger in Amsterdam,[55] who was a celebrity in his field. Ungers' purchases became the core of a collection of more than 12 000 volumes that enjoys a legendary reputation among architecture lovers. Amongst specialised private libraries presumably only that of art and architecture historian Werner Oechslin in Einsiedeln (though much larger) can be compared with it.[56] Incidentally, it is hard to believe that Ungers was able to read Vitruvius and Alberti fluently in Latin. He was definitely unable to decipher the Russian-language literature of Soviet constructivism, which he also collected. Of course, true believers also do not receive the beneficial effects of relics by rational means.

From the building of his first house to the building of his library OMU had come a long way. After his return from the U.S., contacts with clients in Germany initially proved very slow to establish. A turning point came with the programmatic construction of the Deutsches Architekturmuseum in Frankfurt am Main (1979–84), which he owed to the museum's director Heinrich Klotz, and of the simultaneous Badische Landesbibliothek in Karlsruhe. The Deutsches Architekturmuseum was a prestigious project which required the architect to address the existing historical buildings, with a double villa from the period immediately preceding World War I.[56] First and foremost, the commission to design an institution dedicated to architecture gave him the opportunity to have a critical look at the basic principles of construction, such as the motif of encasing and of the morphological development of forms.

The Badisches Landesbibliothek was built across from the Church of St. Stephan, designed by the Karlsruhe architect Friedrich Weinbrenner (1766–1826), whose classicist discipline and clarity was of benefit to Ungers' design. Ten years later Ungers set about creating an even more disciplined and austere, though also incom-

seine Bibliothek, den Raum- und Nutzungstyp des *studiolo*. *Studioli* waren der Meditation und dem Studium gewidmete Kabinette, die an den italienischen Fürstenhöfen des Quattro- und Cinquecento aufkamen und mit wissenschaftlichen Instrumenten, Kunstwerken, Bizarrerien und Büchern ausgestattet waren.[58] Manche Kunstwerke waren eigens für den jeweiligen Standort angefertigte Aufträge. Das galt auch für den Neubau an der Quadrather Straße, der die Bücher und die Arbeitsplätze des Ehepaars Ungers aufnahm.

Zugleich war das Konzept vom Gegenteil einer abgeschiedenen Arbeitszelle bestimmt, vom Bild der Stadt. Denn in seiner Andersartigkeit vervollständigte der Bibliothekskubus die kleine Baugruppe zur Metapher der Stadt. Man wandert fasziniert durch ein privates, aber urban gedachtes Miniaturreich. Städte müssen nicht einer einheitlichen Regel folgen, sie erlauben, ja verlangen die Heterotopie. Sie vereinen unterschiedliche Räume an einem einzigen Ort und führen zusammen, was eigentlich nicht vereinbar scheint. Im neuen Bibliotheksbau werden Bücher und Bilder studiert, werden Verhandlungen abgewickelt und – im Untergeschoß – Archivarbeiten betrieben. Ungers liebte es, als Vergleichsbeispiel die *villa suburbana* Kaiser Hadrians bei Tivoli (118–134 n. Chr.) zu zitieren. Auch sie ist nicht »Villa« im Sinne eines herrschaftlichen Einzelgebäudes, sondern eine Palaststadt – sogar mit einem Bau, der lange Zeit als Bibliothek galt.

Formal stellt der Kubus in seiner geometrischen Unerbittlichkeit das ganz Andere, das *alter ego* zum Formenkatarakt des älteren Hauses dar. Der »lange Weg« vom Eingang an der Belvederestraße her setzt sich, akzentuiert durch ein pyramidales Oberlicht, im südlichen Flügel des Bibliotheksumgangs fort und wird so vollends zur inneren »Straße« mit unterschiedlichen »Adressen«. An der Quadrather Straße entstand ein kleiner Platz mit einem zweiten Eingang. Ihn markieren eine kleine Baumgruppe und, wie ein schmächtig geratener Campanile, eine oben abgetreppte Betonstele des Kölner Bildhauers und Düsseldorfer Akademieprofessors Hubert Kiecol – ein Werk der Natur und eines der Kunst. Für OMU verkörperten beide in ihrem Wechselbezug das Prinzip der Transformation. Das eine, bedauernswerte, Exemplar der beiden Bäume mußte deswegen stets auf die Form einer Stele, einer Naturstele, beschnitten werden.

Das Haus im Haus

Erstaunlich bleibt, wie viele Variationen die Festlegung auf eine einfache stereometrische Form, den Würfel, offen läßt. Es existieren Hunderte von Skizzen, in denen Ungers die Möglichkeiten wie unter Zwang durchprobierte. Er hat die Fassaden des Bücherturms immer wieder geändert, in der Zeichnung, am Modell und noch am Rohbau. In der Gadenzone hatte er eine Fensterreihe vorgesehen, die er wieder zumauern ließ. Schließlich wählte er kleine quadratische Luken knapp unter dem Mauerabschluß, die lediglich der Entlüftung dienen. Nichts ist schwieriger als das Einfache.

Innerhalb der asketischen Außenfigur entfaltet sich eine unvermutete Vielfalt von Raumeindrücken. Tageslicht fällt durch vier Laternenaufsätze ein. Große historische Bibliotheken wurden gern mit zentralisierenden Kuppeln als Zeichen universalen Wissens ausgezeichnet. Ungers beließ es bei den gläsernen Aufsätzen als angemessenen Erleuchtungen. Doch das Licht fällt auch hier von oben in eine umgrenzte Welt des Wissens. Zusätzliche, aber gedämpfte Helligkeit verbreiten die acht Türausschnitte, die ihrerseits Tageslicht aus dem glasüberdeckten äußeren Umgang empfangen. Künstliches Licht kommt aus Punktstrahlern in den Deckenfeldern des inneren Umgangs und der Gesamtdecke. Für den optischen Eindruck schließen sie sich zu einem kleinen Lichter-Universum zusammen.

Was ist aus der Forderung des Manifests von 1960 geworden, Architektur müsse Einordnung in das Vorhandene, Akzentsetzung und Überhöhung des Ortes, Erkennen des *genius loci* bieten? Hätte man die protestierenden Nachbarn befragt, so hätten sie eine »Einordnung in das Vorhandene« gewiß nicht wahrgenommen. Sie fanden das fensterlose Monument eher bedrohlich, sahen in ihm Mausoleum, Bunker oder Transformatorenhaus. Die schwarze, würfelförmige Kaaba zu Mekka war noch der schmeichelhafteste Vergleich. Immerhin handelt es sich um einen Wallfahrtsort für Architekturpilger. Ungers und Frau Lo suchten die Mißvergnügten durch geführte Einladungen zu beschwichtigen.

In der Außenansicht setzte der Umgang des Bücherturms die früheren Gartenmauern fort, die dafür höher gezogen wurden. An den unterschiedlichen Farbtönen der Ziegel, auch aus den in unterschiedlicher Höhe liegenden Rollschichten lassen sich die Spuren des Eingriffs verfolgen.[59] Die Traufhöhe des Wohngebäudes wurde vom Neubau eingehalten; so viel Rücksicht herrschte denn doch.

Außen sind die sichtbaren Seitenwände des Kubus mit dunklem Eifelbasalt verkleidet, und die Dachfläche ebenso. Wenn die Fassade dem Regen ausgesetzt ist, färbt sie sich von Anthrazit nach Schwarz, wandelt also ihr Äußeres mit den Wetterverhältnissen. Der vulkanische Stein spielt zwar nicht auf Müngersdorfer Nachbarschaften an, wohl aber auf das Waldgebirge im Südwesten und damit auf die biographische Laufbahn von OMU. Sie verlief, wie er kokettierte, nicht anders als die antike Wasserleitung, von der römisch besiedelten Eifel zur *Colonia Claudia Ara Agrippinensium*.[60] In dieser Fassung war es eine stark gekürzte Version der Ungersschen Vita, die ihn immerhin an viele andere Orte Europas und der USA geführt hat.

Ein surreales Moment ist dem Eindruck der Bibliothek beigemischt. Eine mächtige, freitragende Wendeltreppe aus dunkel gebeiztem Buchenholz, fast zu groß für diesen Raum, führt auf die Empore. Es ist vorzügliche Handwerkerarbeit, die in vorausgehenden Versionen auch einläufig gerade, zylindrisch oder achteckig angedacht und in Modellen erprobt worden war. Ihr Anschluß an die Bücherempore wurde vor Ort entschieden, die bereits realisierte Treppenspindel dabei um neunzig Grad gedreht. Wie ein vorzeitliches Lebewesen krümmt sich das gewundene Gebilde nun und nimmt fast ein Viertel des Raumvolumens ein. Vollends in eine andere Welt führen die zwölf aufgesockelten Gipsabgüsse eines antiken Apollokopfes (1989), die der schottische Konzeptkünstler Ian Hamilton Finlay mit den hingerichteten Jakobiner-Freunden Robespierres assoziierte. Eigentlich hätten acht Köpfe für die acht Interkolumnien der Galerie gereicht. Aber da der Set nun einmal zwölf umfaßte, stehen jetzt zusätzlich vier Exemplare hinter den vier mittleren Emporenstützen.

Finlays *The Twelve Who Ruled* verkörpern das Surreale, das in dem Ungersschen Interessenmix auch ein Ingredienz ist. Beispielsweise schreitet in seinen Wettbewerbsentwürfen für das Kölner Wallraf-Richartz-Mu-

23. Oswald Mathias Ungers, Haus Belvederestraße 60, Köln-Müngersdorf. Seiteneingang an der Quadrather Straße mit einer Stele aus Beton von Hubert Kiecol, 1991. (Photo: Dieter Leistner.)
24. Oswald Mathias Ungers, Wallraf-Richartz-Museum, Köln, Wettbewerbsentwurf, 1975. Perspektiven der zentralen Achse.

23. Oswald Mathias Ungers, Haus Belvederestraße 60, Köln-Müngersdorf. Side entrance on Quadrather Straße with a concrete stele by Hubert Kiecol, 1991. (Photo: Dieter Leistner.)
24. Oswald Mathias Ungers, Wallraf-Richartz-Museum, Cologne, competition project, 1975. Perspective views of the central axis.

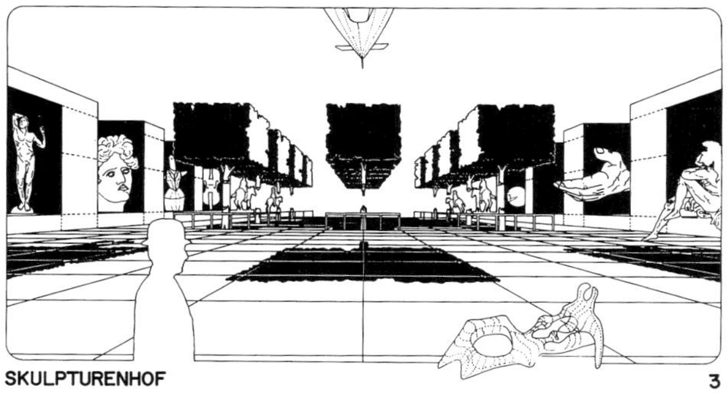

SKULPTURENHOF 3

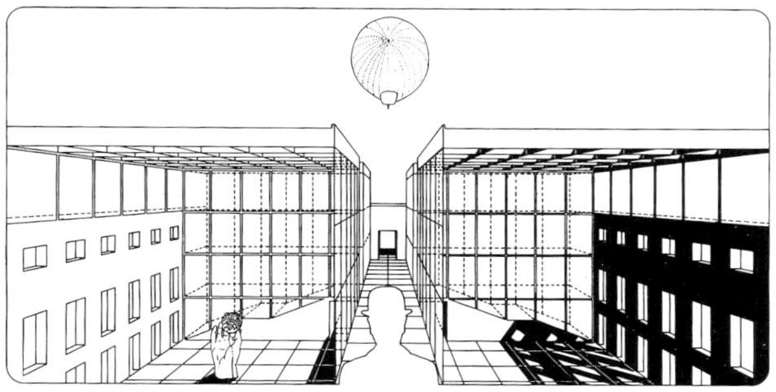

EINGANGSHALLE 2

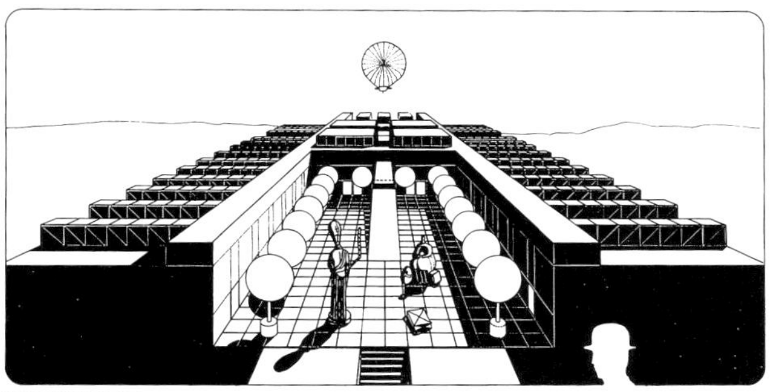

MUSEUMSHOF I

parably smaller, building for his own collection of books. Ungers had a vision for his library – a spatial and usage type referred to as a *studiolo*. *Studioli* were small rooms dedicated to meditation and study found at Italian courts of the Quattro- and Cinquecento and equipped with scientific instruments, artworks, curios and books.[58] Some of the artworks were specifically commissioned for the particular location. This was also true of the new construction on Quadrather Straße that housed the books and workplaces of the Ungerses.

At the same time the concept was dictated by the very opposite of a secluded work cell, the image of the city. For in its otherness the library cube completed the small complex of buildings into a metaphor of the city. Fascinated, you wander through a miniature realm that is private but thought of as urban. Cities do not have to follow a uniform rule, they allow, indeed they demand heterotopy. They combine different rooms in a single place and bring together what actually does not seem compatible. In the new library building, books and pictures are studied, negotiations are concluded and – on the ground floor – archival work goes on. Ungers loved to cite the *villa suburbana* of Emperor Hadrian near Tivoli (118–134 CE) as a comparable example. It, too, is not a »villa« in the sense of an individual stately house, but a city of palaces – even including a building that for a long time passed for a library.

From a formal point of view the cube, geometrically intransigent, represents that which is completely other, the *alter ego* of the older house's cataract of forms. The »long path« from the Belvederestraße entrance continues, accentuated by a pyramid-shaped skylight, in the south wing of the library's gallery and thus finally becomes an interior »street« with various »addresses«. On Quadrather Straße a small open area was created with a second entrance. This is marked by a small group of trees and, like a slender campanile, a concrete stele whose top is stepped, by the Cologne sculptor and professor of the Düsseldorf Arts Academy Hubert Kiecol – a work of nature and one of art. For OMU these two in their interconnection embodied the principle of transformation. That was why, regrettably, one of the trees constantly had to be pruned to the shape of a stele, a »natural stele«.

The house within a house

What is amazing is how many variations the choice of a geometric form, the cube, leaves open. There are hundreds of sketches in which Ungers tried out the possibilities as if under compulsion. He kept changing the façades of the tower of books over and over, in the drawing, on the model and even while in construction. In the clerestorey zone he had planned to have a row of windows that he then walled up again. Finally he chose small square hatches just below the wall ending, used only for ventilation. Nothing is more difficult than simplicity.

Inside the ascetic exterior an unexpected variety of spatial impressions unfolds. Daylight falls through four skylights. A favourite feature of large historical libraries were centralising cupolas, symbols of universal knowledge. Ungers was content with using the glass skylights to provide appropriate lighting. But here too the light falls from above into a circumscribed world of knowledge. Additional, yet muted light comes from the eight door openings, which in turn receive daylight from the glass-covered exterior gallery. Artificial light comes from spotlights in the ceiling panels of the interior gallery and the ceiling as a whole. Together they create the optical impression of a small universe of lights.

What became of the demand, in the 1960 manifesto, that architecture must fit into an existing setting, must accent and intensify the place, recognise the *genius loci*? The neighbours were up in arms. Had they been asked, they would certainly not have agreed that the library »fitted into the existing setting«. To them, the windowless monument looked menacing: they saw it as a mausoleum, bunker or transformer station. Perhaps the most flattering comparison was to the black, cube-shaped Kaaba in Mecca. After all, the library *is* a destination for architecture pilgrims. Ungers and Frau Lo tried to appease disgruntled neighbours by inviting them to take guided tours.

In the exterior view the gallery of the tower of books continued the former garden walls, which therefore were raised. It is possible to trace the intervention by the different shades of colour of the bricks, and also by the courses of bricks lying at different levels.[59] The eaves of the new building had the same height as those of the residence; at least there was that much consideration.

On the outside, the visible side walls of the cube are clad with dark Eifel basalt, and so is the roof. When the façade is exposed to rain, its colour changes from anthracite to black; in other words, its appearance changes with the weather. While the volcanic rock does not allude to local Müngersdorf geological features, it does evoke the wooded mountain range in the southwest and thus OMU's own career. As Ungers playfully suggested, his career followed the same course as the ancient aqueduct, from the Eifel, settled by the Romans, to the *Colonia Claudia Ara Agrippinensium*.[60] It was thus a highly abbreviated version of Ungers' life, which, to be sure, also brought him to many other places in Europe and the United States.

There is something surreal about the design of the library. A massive, cantilevered spiral staircase made of dark stained beech wood, almost too large for this space, leads to the gallery. This is outstanding craftsmanship, which in preceding versions had also been conceived of as a single-flight, straight staircase, or as cylindrical or octagonal, and had been tried out in models. Its connection to the book gallery was decided in situ, and the newel, which had already been realised, was rotated by 90 degrees. The spiral structure now writhes like an antediluvian creature, taking up almost a quarter of the space. We are transported into an entirely different world by the twelve plaster casts of an ancient head of Apollo (1989), raised on plinths, which the Scottish conceptual artist Ian Hamilton Finlay associated with the executed Jacobin friends of Robespierre. Actually eight heads would have sufficed for the eight intercolumniations of the gallery. But since the set included twelve, an additional four copies now stand behind the gallery's four middle columns.

Finlay's *The Twelve Who Ruled* embody the surreal element that is one of Ungers' many interests as well. For instance, in Ungers' competition entries for the Cologne Wallraf-Richartz-Museum (1975) the silhouette of René Magritte's *Man in the Bowler Hat* walks across squares and terraces as a ubiquitous presence. A year later, for a Hans Hollein exhibition in the Cooper-Hewitt Museum, New York, Ungers contributed an installation of urban

seum (1975) die Silhouette von René Magrittes *Mann mit der Melone* als allgegenwärtiger Betrachter über Plätze und Terrassen. Ein Jahr später steuerte Ungers zu einer Ausstellung Hans Holleins im New Yorker Cooper-Hewitt Museum eine Installation von Stadtmetaphern in einem langen Raumschlauch bei, in dem der Magritte-Mann in schwarzen Holzsilhouetten aus Wand und Boden herauszutreten scheint. Surreale Wirkung registrierte er, »wenn zwei gegensätzliche Wirklichkeiten aufeinander treffen«, so bei Le Corbusiers »Offener Hand« in Chandigarh oder in den Architekturbildern Giorgio De Chiricos.[61]

Andere Kunstwerke in der Müngersdorfer Bibliothek beziehen sich auf das Metier des Architekten. Acht Gipsreliefs von historischen wie zeitgenössischen Städten wie Karlsruhe, Trier oder Berlin, angefertigt in Alabastergips von Bernd Grimm, wurden in Supraporten eingelassen. In den obersten Fächern der Bücherregale stehen kleine Modelle aus Architekturgeschichte oder Ungersscher Produktion. Wie der Bücherbestand unterstreichen sie den enzyklopädischen Anspruch – und wie die Büchersammlung können auch sie nur die Abbreviatur einer Enzyklopädie sein, nicht diese selbst in ihrer utopischen Vollständigkeit. In die quadratischen Gipstafeln knapp unter der Decke hat Gerhard Merz einen Auszug aus Paul Valérys fiktivem Dialog *Eupalinos oder Der Architekt* geschnitten, ein Text, der Ungers wichtig war.

Katarakt und Kubus, Frühwerk der späten 1950er und Spätwerk von 1990, aufmerksamkeitsheischendes Architekturmanifest und abweisende Geschlossenheit der geometrischen Figur, ein Maximum an individueller Künstlerfreiheit und ein Maximum an archetypischer Ideenfixierung – trotz aller Unterschiede machen die beiden kontrastierenden Formate doch gemeinsame Sache. Den wechselseitig sich ausschließenden Gegensatz hat Ungers nicht ausgespielt, die Kunst der Fuge nicht dramatisiert. Bildende Kunst besetzt beide Haushälften. Ziegelstein bleibt ein maßbildendes Material auch im neuen Trakt.

Begriffe aus dem Gieselmann-Ungers-Manifest treffen auch jetzt, dreißig Jahre später, noch zu: Akzentsetzung und Überhöhung, Asymmetrie statt Symmetrie, Überraschung statt Vorhersehbarkeit. Und ebenso: »An die Stelle des Gegenüber-Seins das Darin-Sein«, »Architektur ist Einhüllung und Bergung«.[62] Das Ganze, Altbau wie Neubau, geht auf in einem Labyrinth, das vielfältig ist wie eine kleine Stadt, in der auch das Heterogene aufeinander trifft – »eine Welt voller Widersprüche, Illusionen und Wirklichkeiten, die das ganze Spektrum vom Bild der Architektur, der Fiktion bis zur Wirklichkeit der Funktion wiedergibt.«[63]

Ein Bildkomplex, der OMUs Phantasie immer wieder beschäftigte, war das Haus im Haus, das Objekt im Objekt, die Puppe in der Puppe, die Stadt in der Stadt. »Das Thema vom Haus im Haus entspricht einem Raum, der durch mehrere Hüllen geschützt ist, oder – anders ausgedrückt – mehrere Raumhüllen umgeben einen im Kern liegenden Raum.«[64] Das Prinzip »Haus im Haus«, am prominentesten realisiert im Frankfurter Deutschen Architekturmuseum, gilt auch für den Müngersdorfer Bau. Ein weiß gestrichenes kubisches Gerüst aus Stahlbetonpfosten und -bindern, 6 x 6 x 6 m, steckt in der Hülle der schwarzen inneren Bücherregale und der Außenwand. Der Korpus der Bibliothek wiederum steckt in der Hülle eines eingeschossigen Umgangs. Schließlich steckt der gesamte Bücherbau in der Masse des vielteiligen Hausvolumens. Zwei scheinbar widersprüchliche Maximen wußte Ungers durchaus miteinander zu verbinden: einerseits die Forderung, mit der Architektur Bilder und Themen zu setzen, andererseits den im Alter zunehmenden Hang zur Abstraktion und die Beschränkung auf ein Minimum – allerdings ein äußerst luxuriöses Minimum. »Ich suche die reine, gegenstandslose Form.« [65]

So hat Ungers diese Erweiterung seines Hauses und seines Denkens auch nicht als Abschluß betrachtet, sondern als Station einer Suchbewegung. Kaum standen das Haus Glashütte in der Eifel und die Ergänzung des Hauses Belvederestraße durch die Bibliothek, beschäftigten ihn schon Gedanken an den Bau eines dritten – oder wenn man die Bibliothek als eigenen Bau mitzählt: vierten – Hauses, diesmal wieder in der Nähe, am Kämpchensweg 58 (1993–94). Den dreischiffigen, zweistöckigen Flachbau hat Francesco Dal Co eine *casa senza qualità* genannt.[66] Ein Haus ohne Eigenschaften: Diese Formel machte sich OMU zu eigen.

Natürlich besitzt es Eigenschaften, sehr ausgeprägte sogar: keinen eindeutigen Eingang, keine Mittel- und Symmetrieachse, stattdessen vier Fenstertüren an beiden Längsseiten; doppelschalige Längs- und Innenwände, in denen sich auf dem Wege zur Großen Ordnung alles Unerwünschte verbergen läßt, von der Kochwand über Treppen bis zu WCs, Gästegarderobe und dem Hundekörbchen. Die Fassaden mit ihren minimalen Daten – flächenbündige Fensterausschnitte, Enkaustoputz – sind durch ein quadriertes Raster geregelt. Als sichtbares Markenzeichen bleibt diesmal aber das Quadrat aus dem Spiel; alle Fenster sind hochrechteckig.

Als Vorbilder in der Organisation des basilikalen Grundrisses hat Ungers Palladio, Schinkel und Mies van der Rohe genannt.[67] Der Minimalismus der Erscheinung bleibt unübertroffen: »nur Haut, reine Form, keine Metapher, keine narrativen Anspielungen. Glatt, abgeschliffen, präzise, die Grundform – nicht mehr.«[68] Hätte der Schüler Eiermanns sich im Alter zum Diktum seines Lehrers bekannt? »Ich möchte ausdrücklich betonen«, schrieb Eiermann 1961, »daß mir nicht an einer Architektur liegt, die durch ständige Produktion von Neuheiten und Überraschungen Sensationen hervorzurufen sucht. Meine Arbeit besteht darin, bestimmte Erfahrungen und Kenntnisse, die ich im Laufe meiner Arbeit gesammelt habe, als Standard, d.h. mit dem Begriff der Allgemeingültigkeit versehen, weiterzuentwickeln und sie zur Vollendung zu bringen«.[69]

Aber die Motivlage war beim späten Ungers eine andere. Es ging ihm nicht um die Entwicklung eines Produkts, das durch ständige Verbesserung typologische Bestform erreicht und damit anwendbar für Produktion und Reproduktion wird. Ihm ging es am Ende seines Architektenlebens um die möglichst große Nähe zur Idee des Hauses, unter Verzicht auf jede störende Ablenkung, unter Preisgabe alles dessen, was es an die reale Welt mit ihren allzu menschlichen Kompromissen band, um reine Architektur. Von der produktiven Überraschungsästhetik führte die Reihe der Ungersschen Privathäuser zur rigorosen Reduktionsästhetik. Einer, der es wissen wollte, machte die Probe, wie viel man von Architektur wegnehmen kann, ohne daß sie aufhört, Architektur zu sein.

metaphors in a long tube of space in which the Magritte man seems to emerge from the wall and floor in the shape of black wooden silhouettes. He noted a surreal effect »when two contrasting realities come into conflict«, as in Le Corbusier's »Open Hand« in Chandigarh or in Giorgio De Chirico's architectural paintings.[61]

Other artworks in the Müngersdorf library refer to the architect's profession. Eight plaster reliefs of both historical and contemporary cities such as Karlsruhe, Trier or Berlin, made of alabaster gypsum by Bernd Grimm, were installed in supraportas. In the topmost compartments of the bookshelves there are small models from architectural history or Ungers' own production. Like the holdings of the library, they emphasize its encyclopaedic aspiration – and like the collection of books they too can be merely the abbreviation of an encyclopaedia, not the encyclopaedia itself in its utopian comprehensiveness. On the square plaster tablets just below the ceiling, Gerhard Merz carved an excerpt from Paul Valéry's fictitious dialogue *Eupalinos, or The Architect*, a text that was important for Ungers.

Cataract and cube, the early work of the late 1950s and the late work of 1990, an attention-grabbing architectural manifesto and the cold, closed geometric figure, a maximum of individual artistic freedom and a maximum of archetypal idées fixes – in spite of all differences the two contrasting formats nevertheless make common cause. Ungers did not exploit this mutually exclusive contrast, nor did he dramatise the art of the fugue. Works of fine art are displayed in both halves of the house. Brick continues to be an important material in the new wing as well.

Concepts from the Gieselmann-Ungers manifesto still apply today, thirty years later: accentuation and exaggeration, asymmetry instead of symmetry, surprise instead of predictability. And also: »Instead of being opposite, being in there«, »[the essence of] architecture is to envelop and shelter«.[62] The entire complex, the old building and the new, is fused in a labyrinth that is multifaceted like a little town, in which heterogeneous features also come together – »a world full of contradictions, illusions and realities that reflects the entire spectrum of the image of architecture, from the fiction to the reality of the function.«[63]

One complex of images that preoccupied OMU's imagination again and again was the house within the house, the object within the object, the doll within the doll, the town within the town. »The theme of the house within the house is that of a space protected by several envelopes, or – in other words – several envelopes surround a space at the core.«[64] The principle of the »house within a house«, most prominently exemplified by the Deutsches Architekturmuseum in Frankfurt am Main, also applies to the Müngersdorf building. A white-painted cubical framework of reinforced concrete pillars and girders, 6 x 6 x 6 m, is contained in the envelope of the black interior bookshelves and the exterior wall. The body of the library in turn is contained in the envelope of a one-storey gallery. Finally, the entire library building is contained in the mass of the multipartite volume of the house. Ungers was able successfully to combine two seemingly contradictory maxims: on the one hand the demand that architecture set images and themes, on the other his increasing tendency as he grew older toward abstraction and toward restriction to a minimum – though admittedly a very luxurious minimum. »I am looking for pure, abstract form.« [65]

Thus Ungers also did not consider this expansion of his house and of his thinking as a conclusion, but as one phase of an exploration. No sooner had the Glashütte house in the Eifel and the expansion of the Belvederestraße-house library been completed, than he was already thinking of building a third – or, if you count the library as a separate building, a fourth house, this time nearby again, on Kämpchensweg 58 (1993–94). Francesco Dal Co called the flat, triple-nave, two-storey building a *casa senza qualità*.[66] A house without qualities: a formula that OMU made peculiarly his own.

Naturally it does have qualities, and very distinctive ones at that: no explicit entrance, no central axis and axis of symmetry, instead there are four French doors in both long sides; double-shell longitudinal and interior walls in which, to achieve radical order, all undesirable items can be concealed, from the cooking area to stairs to toilets, guest cloakroom and the dog basket. The façades with their minimal data – flush mount windows, encaustic plaster – are regulated by a squared grid. This time, however, Ungers' visible trademark, the square, is not part of the design; all the windows are upright rectangular.

As his models in the organisation of the basilica-like ground plan, Ungers named Palladio, Schinkel and Mies van der Rohe.[67] The minimalism of the design has never been excelled: »nothing but membrane, pure form, no metaphor, no narrative allusions. Smooth, stripped down, precise, the basic form – no more.«[68] Could it be that in his old age Eiermann's pupil declared his support for his teacher's dictum? »I should like to expressly state«, wrote Eiermann in 1961, »that an architecture that seeks to provoke sensations by the constant production of novelties and surprises does not appeal to me. My work consists in further developing certain experiences and insights I have gathered in the course of my career as a standard, i.e., as something provided with universal validity, and to bring them to perfection«.[69]

Ungers' late work, however, had a different motivation. He was not interested in developing a product that reaches its optimum typological form through continuous improvement and can thus be used for production and reproduction. At the end of his career as an architect he was interested in coming as close as possible to the concept of the house, renouncing all distractions, abandoning everything that bound it to the real world with its all too human compromises – pure architecture. From a productive aesthetics of surprise, the series of Ungers' private residences led to a rigorous aesthetics of reduction. Eager to find out, Ungers explored how much one can take away from an architectural structure for it still to be architecture.

Anmerkungen

Abgekürzte Literaturangaben vgl. Literaturverzeichnis.

[1] Ungers 1999, S. 6–8.
[2] Belvederestraße 60 (1958–59) und Kämpchensweg 58 (1994–95), Köln-Müngersdorf; Glashütte bei Utscheid im Eifelkreis Bitburg-Prüm (1986–88). Das Haus Belvederestraße steht unter Denkmalschutz und gehört dem internationalen Netzwerk »Iconic Houses« an. Eigentümer der Häuser Belvederestraße und Glashütte ist die Erbengemeinschaft Ungers; die Bibliothek ist seit 1990 im Besitz der Stiftung Ungers Archiv für Architekturwissenschaft (UAA). Das UAA versteht sich als Forschungszentrum. Es verwaltet den Nachlaß von Oswald Mathias Ungers, veranstaltet Vorträge, Ausstellungen und Führungen und arbeitet mit Hochschulen und Institutionen des In- und Auslands zusammen. Bibliothek und Sammlung sind der interessierten Öffentlichkeit zugänglich.
[3] Ungers 1999, S. 6, 12 f.
[4] Visiting Critic, bzw. Professor: 1965, 1967, 1975–86 Cornell University, Ithaca, 1973, 1978 Harvard University, Cambridge, Mass., 1974–75 University of California, Los Angeles.
[5] Haus Emil Lettré, Rüsternallee, Berlin-Charlottenburg, Architekt Eduard Pfeiffer (1922–23). Cepl 2007, S. 160 f., 304 ff.
[6] Ungers 1999, S. 8, 14.
[7] Giorgio Vasari, *Le Vite de'piu eccellenti pittori, scultori e architettori*, Florenz 1550, zit. nach der Ausgabe von Gaetano Milanesi, 1878–85, Bd. II, S. 78.
[8] Vgl. Schwarz 1990.
[9] Bezeichnenderweise engagierte sich Ungers für die Rekonstruktion einer in Holsthum, Südeifel, ergrabenen römischen Villa. Die Rekonstruktion blieb Projekt.
[10] Schwarz (Hg.) 1989, S. 55, 64–68. – John Summerson, *A New Description of Sir John Soane's Museum*, London, 1955, 1972[3].
[11] Soane besaß auch einen umgebauten Landsitz, Pitzhanger Manor, Ealing, erworben und umgebaut 1800–02.
[12] Stabenow 2000, hier und im folgenden, S. 19–39.
[13] »Hoch oder flach? Interview mit Egon Eiermann«, in: *Der Erfolg, aktuelle Büro- und Betriebsorganisation,* 17 (1968), 3, S. 25, zit. nach: Immo Boyken, »Die Architektur Egon Eiermanns aus der Zeit nach dem Zweiten Weltkrieg«, in: Wulf Schirmer (Hg.), *Egon Eiermann 1904 bis 1970. Bauten und Projekte*, Stuttgart 1984, S. 67.
[14] Cepl 2007, S. 32–33.
[15] In einem Empfehlungsschreiben an den Kulturkreis im Bundesverband der Deutschen Industrie vom 26. 3. 1957 schreibt Schwarz: »Unger [sic] ist ein jüngerer Kölner Architekt, der einige bildschöne Bauten errichtet hat, aber trotzdem nicht recht hochkommt, weil es ihm nicht gelungen ist, Verständnis für seine künstlerische Eigenart zu erwecken.« (Nachlaß Rudolf Schwarz, Köln.)
[16] Das »X« bezieht sich auf den in Vorbereitung befindlichen zehnten (X.) Kongreß der CIAM.
[17] Mündliche Mitteilung von Ungers. Vgl. auch Francis Strauven, *Aldo van Eyck. The Shape of Relativity,* Amsterdam 1998, S. 256.
[18] Reinhard Gieselmann, Oswald Mathias Ungers, »X. Triennale Mailand«, in: *Baukunst und Werkform*, 7 (1954), 10, S. 589–595.
[19] Wolfram Hagspiel, Ruth Mader, »Helmut Goldschmidt. Portrait eines ungewöhnlichen Kölner Architekten«, in: *polis. Zeitschrift für Architektur und Stadtplanung*, 12 (2000), 2, S. 34–39; Cepl 2007, S. 35.
[20] Mehrfamilienhaus Hültzstraße, Köln-Braunsfeld, 1951; Mehrfamilienhaus und Kleiderfabrik Aachener Straße, Köln-Braunsfeld, 1951.
[21] Mehrfamilienhäuser u. a. Mauenheimer Straße, Köln-Nippes, 1957–59; Institut zur Erlangung der Hochschulreife, Oberhausen, 1953–58; Mehrfamilienhaus Aachener Straße, 1958; Mehrfamilien- und Geschäftshaus, Hansaring, Köln, 1959. In: Ungers 1951–1990, 1991. – Kieren 1994.
[22] Die Charta wurde auf der Tagung *Die funktionelle Stadt* von CIAM-Architekten formuliert, die 1933 auf dem Dampfer *Patris* von Marseille nach Athen fuhren. Le Corbusier veröffentlichte den Text ohne Verfasserangabe 1941 in Paris.
[23] Der Begriff wurde vor allem seit dem Vortrag diskutiert, den der Schweizer Sozial- und Wirtschaftswissenschaftler Edgar Salin 1960 auf dem Deutschen Städtetag in Augsburg hielt.
[24] Leone Battista Alberti (1404–1472), *De re aedificatoria*, 1443–52, hg. von Giovanni Orlandi, *L'architettura*, Mailand 1966, S. 65, 399.
[25] Ungers 1991, S. 45–65.
[26] Ungers 1999, S. 16.
[27] Ungers 1999, S. 8.
[28] Berechnung von Bernd Grimm.
[29] Planungsgemeinschaft Paulskirche, *Denkschrift zur Fortsetzung des Wiederaufbaus der Paulskirche Frankfurt/Main*, April 1960, Nachlaß Schwarz, Köln. Vgl. Pehnt 2011, S. 169–186.
[30] Zur Publikationsgeschichte des Manifestes: Cepl 2007, S. 68–75. Es war spätestens seit seiner Veröffentlichung in Ulrich Conrads (Hg.), *Programme und Manifeste zur Architektur des 20. Jahrhunderts*, Braunschweig, 1964 und öfter, S. 158 f. einer breiteren Öffentlichkeit zugänglich. – Gieselmann 2007.
[31] Ungers 1983, S. 13.
[32] Gespräche mit Oswald Mathias Ungers seit 1981.
[33] Johann Wolfgang von Goethe, *Die Metamorphose der Pflanzen*, in: *Goethes Werke*, Hamburger Ausgabe, Band 13, Hamburg 1962[4].
[34] *Rede von Herrn Prof. O. M. Ungers anläßlich der Verleihung der Goethe-Plakette der Stadt Frankfurt am Main am 4.3.2002*, Typoskript, UAA, S. 2.
[35] Oswald Mathias Ungers in einem Gespräch mit Nikolaus Kuhnert, »Detail: Das Tüpfelchen auf dem i«, in: *Arch+* 87 (1986), S. 38. Hinweis bei Cepl 2007, S. 68 ff., Anm. 1. Vgl. Pehnt 2011.
[36] Gerhard Kabierske, »›Sie wollten Funktion – ich: Struktur und Atmosphäre‹. Zu Leben und Werk von Reinhard Gieselmann«, in: Gieselmann 2007, S. 15.
[37] Oswald Mathias Ungers »Eigenes Wohnhaus in Köln-Müngersdorf«, in: *Bauwelt*, 51 (1960), 8. S. 213–215.
[38] Franco Borsi, Giovanni Klaus König. *Architettura dell' Espressionismo*. Genua, Paris, 1967. S. 9 f. – Rossi 1960.
[39] Banhams Paradebeispiel: die Secondary School in Hunstanton, Norfolk, von Alison und Peter Smithson, 1949–54. Banham 1966, S.19 f., 32–40.
[40] Banham 1966, S.125 f.
[41] Ausführliche Darstellung in Cepl 2007, S. 59–83.
[42] S. Giedion, *Raum, Zeit, Architektur*, Ravensburg 1965, S. 22.
[43] *Bauen und Wohnen*, 15 (1960), 9. S. 302.
[44] Nikolaus Pevsner, »Modern Architecture and the Historian, or the Return of Historicism«, in: *Journal of the Royal Institute of British Architects*, 3 (1961), S. 230 to 240, – dt.: »Wiederkehr des Historismus«, in: *Architektur und Design, Von der Romantik zur Sachlichkeit*, München 1971, S. 500, 502.
[45] Cepl 2007, S. 90–120. Dem Kollegen bin ich für die Überlassung von Material zum Thema Ungers und der Expressionismus dankbar. Ungers behauptete, erst die Einordnung des eigenen Werks durch andere in die Rubrik Neoexpressionismus habe ihn zur Beschäftigung mit dem historischen Expressionismus gebracht (Typoskript und Manuskript ohne Titel, Mai 1964, Archiv für Architekturwissenschaft, Köln, UAA). Pevsners Exkurs zum zeitgenössischen Historismus erschien deutsch zuerst im Oktoberheft 1961 der Zeitschrift *Deutsche Bauzeitung* (Cepl 2007, S. 90). Ulrich Conrads deutete jedoch an, daß Ungers bereits in den späten 1950er Jahren durch einen zu diesem Zeitpunkt noch unveröffentlichten Band von Conrads und Hans G. Sperlich, *Phantastische Architektur*, erschienen erst 1960, mit dem Expressionismus in der Architektur vertraut wurde (Ulrich Conrads an Wolfgang Pehnt, 25. 6. 2010).
[46] Ausstellung »Die gläserne Kette. Visionäre Architekturen aus dem Kreis um Bruno Taut 1919–1920« in Schloß Morsbroich, Leverkusen, 26. 7. bis 8. 9. 1963. – Kat. Leverkusen, Berlin 1963.
[47] Oswald Mathias Ungers, *Rede zur Eröffnung der Finsterlin-Ausstellung in Berlin* (1962). Typoskript, UAA.
[48] F. Borsi, G. K. König, *Architettura dell'Espressionismo*, Genua, Paris 1967, S. 10.
[49] Typoskript, UAA.
[50] S. Giedion, *Raum, Zeit, Architektur*, Ravensburg 1965, S. 307 f.
[51] Oswald Mathias Ungers, *Die Erscheinungsformen des Expressionismus in der Architektur*, 1964. Typoskript, UAA.
[52] Die Modelle befinden sich teils in Glashütte, teils in der Belvederestraße. – Elser 2006, S. 41–53.
[53] Neumeyer 1991, S. 21.
[54] Oswald Mathias Ungers im Gespräch mit Claudia Rudeck, Typoskript, UAA, S. 13, zit. nach: Cepl 2006, S. 38.
[55] Cepl 2006, S. 32.
[56] Erweiterung durch Neubau 2006, Architekt Mario Botta.
[57] Architekt Fritz Geldermann.
[58] Wolfgang Liebenwein, *Studiolo. Die Entstehung eines Raumtyps und seine Entwicklung bis um 1600,* Berlin 1977.
[59] Stabenow 2000, S. 199.
[60] Gespräche mit Ungers seit 1981.
[61] Oswald Mathias Ungers Berliner Berufungsvortrag, 2. Teil, in: Mühlthaler 2006, S.39–40.
[62] Gieselmann, Ungers 1960.
[63] Ungers 1991, S. 216.
[64] Ungers 1983. Darin: »Das Thema der Inkorporation oder ›die Puppe in der Puppe‹«, S. 55–72, zit. 59.
[65] Ungers 1999, S. 8.
[66] Francesco Dal Co, »O. M.Ungers, Schinkel als Erzieher«, in: *Casabella*, 60 (1996), 635, S. 4–11.
[67] Ungers 1999, S. 30, 32. – Das Haus wurde 2011, nach Ungers' Tod, an den Mediziner, Petrarca- und Proust-Sammler Reiner Speck verkauft.
[68] Ungers 1999, S. 8, 11.
[69] Egon Eiermann an Regierungsbaudirektor Carl Mertz, Berlin, 10. 4. 1961. zit.: Immo Boyken, »Die Architektur Eiermanns aus der Zeit nach dem Zweiten Weltkrieg«, in: Wulf Schirmer (Hg.), *Egon Eiermann 1904–1970, Bauten und Projekte*, Stuttgart 1984, S. 70.

Notes

For abbreviated bibliographical references cf. bibliography.

[1] Ungers 1999, pp. 6–8.
[2] Belvederestraße 60 (1958–59) and Kämpchensweg 58 (1994–95), Müngersdorf, Cologne; Glashütte near Utscheid in the Eifel district of Bitburg-Prüm (1986–88). The Belvederestraße house is listed as a historical monument. The Belvederestrasse house is listed as a historical monument and belongs to the international network »Iconic Houses«.The owner of the Belvederestraße and Glashütte houses is the Ungers community of heirs, while the library, since 1990, belongs to the Ungers Archiv für Architekturwissenschaft (UAA). The UAA sees itself as a research center. It administers the estate of Oswald Matthias Ungers, organises lectures, exhibitions and guided tours, and works together with colleges, universities and institutions in Germany and abroad. The library and collection are open to interested members of the general public.
[3] Ungers 1999, pp. 6, 12 f.
[4] Visiting critic and/or professor: 1965, 1967, 1975–86 Cornell University, Ithaca, 1973, 1978 Harvard University, Cambridge, Mass., 1974–75 University of California, Los Angeles.
[5] Emil Lettré House, Rüsternallee, Charlottenburg, Berlin, architect Eduard Pfeiffer (1922–23). Cepl 2007, pp. 160 f., 304 ff.
[6] Ungers 1999, pp. 8, 14.
[7] Giorgio Vasari, *Le Vite de'più eccellenti pittori, scultori e architettori*, Florence 1550, quoted from the edition of Gaetano Milanesi, 1878–85, vol. II, p. 78.
[8] Cf. Schwarz 1990.
[9] Characteristically, Ungers actively supported the reconstruction of a Roman villa excavated in Holsthum, in the southern Eifel. The reconstruction remained a project.
[10] Schwarz (ed.) 1989, pp. 55, 64–68. – John Summerson, *A New Description of Sir John Soane's Museum*, London, 1955, 1972[3].
[11] Soane also owned a rebuilt country seat, Pitzhanger Manor, Ealing, which he purchased and remodeled in 1800–02.
[12] Stabenow 2000, here and subsequently, pp. 19– 39.
[13] »Hoch oder flach? Interview with Egon Eiermann«, in: *Der Erfolg, aktuelle Büro und Betriebsorganisation*, 17 (1968), 3, p. 25, quoted from: Immo Boyken, »Die Architektur Egon Eiermanns aus der Zeit nach dem Zweiten Weltkrieg«, in: Wulf Schirmer (ed.), *Egon Eiermann 1904–1970. Bauten und Projekte*, Stuttgart 1984, p. 67.
[14] Cepl 2007, pp. 32–33.
[15] In a letter of recommendation to the Kulturkreis im Bundesverband der Deutschen Industrie dated 26 March 1957 Schwarz writes: »Unger [sic] is a younger Cologne architect who has designed a number of very beautiful buildings, but nevertheless hasn't quite made his way in the world, because he hasn't succeeded in creating an understanding for his artistic individuality.« (Rudolf Schwarz estate, Cologne.)
[16] The »X« refers to the tenth (X) congress of the CIAM then under preparation.
[17] Verbal statement by Ungers. Cf. also Francis Strauven, *Aldo van Eyck. The Shape of Relativity,* Amsterdam 1998, p. 256.
[18] Reinhard Gieselmann, Oswald Mathias Ungers, »X. Triennale Mailand«, in: *Baukunst und Werkform*, 7 (1954), 10, pp. 589–595.
[19] Wolfram Hagspiel, Ruth Mader, »Helmut Goldschmidt. Portrait eines ungewöhnlichen Kölner Architekten«, in: *polis. Zeitschrift für Architektur und Stadtplanung*, 12 (2000), 2, pp. 34–39; Cepl 2007, p. 35.
[20] Multifamily building in Hültzstraße, Braunsfeld, Cologne, 1951; multi-family building and garment factory in Aachener Straße, Braunsfeld, Cologne, 1951.
[21] Multi-family buildings et al., in Mauenheimer Straße, Nippes, Cologne, 1957–59; Institut zur Erlangung der Hochschulreife, Oberhausen, 1953–58; multifamily building in Aachener Straße, 1958; multifamily and office building on Hansaring, Cologne, 1959. In: Ungers 1951 to 1990, 1991. – Kieren 1994.
[22] The Charter was drawn up at the conference *The functional city* by CIAM architects who were sailing on the steamship *Patris* from Marseille to Athens in 1933. Le Corbusier published the text in Paris in 1941 without giving the name of the authors.
[23] The term was discussed particularly since the lecture given by the Swiss social scientist and economist Edgar Salin in 1960 at the German Association of Cities and Towns in Augsburg.
[24] Leone Battista Alberti (1404–1472), *De re aedificatoria*, 1443–52, ed. by Giovanni Orlandi, *L'architettura*, Milan 1966, pp. 65, 399.
[25] Ungers 1991, pp. 45–65.
[26] Ungers 1999, p. 16.
[27] Ungers 1999, p. 8.
[28] Calculation by Bernd Grimm.
[29] Planungsgemeinschaft Paulskirche, *Denkschrift zur Fortsetzung des Wiederaufbaus der Paulskirche Frankfurt/Main*, April 1960, Schwarz estate, Cologne. Cf. Pehnt 2011, pp. 169–186.
[30] On the publication history of the manifesto: Cepl 2007, pp. 68–75. It was available to a wider public at the latest after its publication in Ulrich Conrads (ed.), *Programme und Manifeste zur Architektur des 20. Jahrhunderts*, Braunschweig, 1964 and passim, p. 158 f. – Gieselmann 2007.
[31] Ungers 1983, p. 13.
[32] Conversations with Oswald Mathias Ungers since 1981.
[33] Johann Wolfgang von Goethe, *Die Metamorphose der Pflanzen*, in: *Goethes Werke*, Hamburg edition, vol. 13, Hamburg 1962[4].
[34] *Rede von Herrn Prof. O. M. Ungers anläßlich der Verleihung der Goethe-Plakette der Stadt Frankfurt am Main am 4. 3. 2002*, typescript, UAA, p. 2.
[35] Oswald Mathias Ungers in a conversation with Nikolaus Kuhnert, *Detail: Das Tüpfelchen auf dem i,* in: Arch+ 87 (1986), p. 38. Reference in Cepl 2007, p. 68 ff., fn. 1. Cf. Pehnt 2011.
[36] Gerhard Kabierske, »›Sie wollten Funktion – ich: Struktur und Atmosphäre‹. Zu Leben und Werk von Reinhard Gieselmann«, in: Gieselmann 2007, p. 15.
[37] Oswald Mathias Ungers, »Eigenes Wohnhaus in Köln-Müngersdorf«, in: *Bauwelt*, 51 (1960), 8, pp. 213 to 215.
[38] Franco Borsi, Giovanni Klaus König. *Architettura dell' Espressionismo*. Genova, Paris, 1967, p. 9 f. – Rossi 1960.
[39] Banham's prime example: the Secondary School in Hunstanton, Norfolk, by Alison and Peter Smithson, 1949–54. Banham 1966, pp. 19 f., 32–40.
[40] Banham 1966, p.125 f.
[41] Detailed description in Cepl 2007, pp. 59–83.
[42] S. Giedion, *Raum, Zeit, Architektur*, Ravensburg 1965, p. 22.
[43] *Bauen und Wohnen*, 15 (1960), 9, p. 302.
[44] Nikolaus Pevsner, »Modern Architecture and the Historian, or the Return of Historicism«, in: *Journal of the Royal Institute of British Architects*, 3 (1961), pp. 230 to 240.
[45] Cepl 2007, pp. 90–120. I am grateful to the colleague for sharing material on the topic of Ungers and Expressionism. Ungers claimed that he had not begun dealing with historical Expressionism until his own work was categorised by others as neo-Expressionism (typescript and untitled manuscript, May 1964, Archiv für Architekturwissenschaft, Cologne (UAA). Pevsner's excursus on contemporary Historicism first appeared in German in the October issue 1961 of the periodical *Deutsche Bauzeitung* (Cepl 2007, p. 90). However, Ulrich Conrads suggested that Ungers already became familiar with Expressionism in architecture in the late 1950s through a volume by Conrads und Hans G. Sperlich, *Phantastische Architektur*, as yet unpublished at the time, which did not appear in print until 1960 (Ulrich Conrads to Wolfgang Pehnt, 25 June 2010).
[46] The exhibition »Die gläserne Kette. Visionäre Architekturen aus dem Kreis um Bruno Taut 1919–1920« in Morsbroich Castle, Leverkusen, 26 July – 8 Sept. 1963. – Cat. Leverkusen, Berlin 1963.
[47] Oswald Mathias Ungers, *Rede zur Eröffnung der Finsterlin-Ausstellung in Berlin* (1962). Typescript, UAA.
[48] F. Borsi, G. K. König, *Architettura dell'Espressionismo*, Genoa, Paris 1967, p. 10.
[49] Typescript, UAA.
[50] S. Giedion, *Raum, Zeit, Architektur*, Ravensburg 1965, p. 307 f.
[51] Oswald Mathias Ungers, *Die Erscheinungsformen des Expressionismus in der Architektur*, 1964. Typescript, UAA.
[52] The models are located partly in Glashütte, partly in Belvederestraße. – Elser 2006, pp. 41–53.
[53] Neumeyer 1991, p. 21.
[54] Oswald Mathias Ungers in conversation with Claudia Rudeck, typescript, UAA, p. 13, quoted from: Cepl 2006, p. 38.
[55] Cepl 2006, p. 32.
[56] Expanded by a new addition in 2006, architect Mario Botta.
[57] Architect Fritz Geldermann.
[58] Wolfgang Liebenwein*, Studiolo. Die Entstehung eines Raumtyps und seine Entwicklung bis um 1600,* Berlin 1977.
[59] Stabenow 2000, p. 199.
[60] Conversations with Ungers since 1981.
[61] Oswald Mathias Ungers' Berlin presentation to the faculty appointment committee, part 2, in: Mühlthaler 2006, pp. 39–40.
[62] Gieselmann, Ungers 1960.
[63] Ungers 1991, p. 216.
[64] Ungers 1983. See: »Das Thema der Inkorporation oder ›die Puppe in der Puppe‹«, pp. 55–72, quot. 59.
[65] Ungers 1999, p. 8.
[66] Francesco Dal Co, »O.M.Ungers. Schinkel als Erzieher«, in: *Casabella*, 60 (1996), 635, pp. 4–11.
[67] Ungers 1999, pp. 30, 32. – In 2011, after Ungers' death, the house was sold to the physician Reiner Speck, a collector of Petrarca and Proust.
[68] Ungers 1999, pp. 8, 11.
[69] Egon Eiermann to Regierungsbaudirektor Carl Mertz, Berlin, 10 April 1961 quoted in: Immo Boyken, »Die Architektur Eiermanns aus der Zeit nach dem Zweiten Weltkrieg«, in: Wulf Schirmer (ed.), *Egon Eiermann 1904 to 1970, Bauten und Projekte*, Stuttgart 1984, p. 70.

Schriften von Oswald Mathias Ungers (Auswahl)
Writings by Oswald Mathias Ungers (selection)

... and Reinhard Gieselmann, »Zu einer neuen Architektur« (1960), in: *Der Monat*, 174, March 1963, p. 96, and in: Ulrich Conrads (ed.), *Programme und Manifeste zur Architektur des 20. Jahrhundert. Bauwelt Fundamente 1*, Berlin 1964, pp. 158 f.

... and Udo Kultermann, *Die gläserne Kette. Visionäre Architekturen aus dem Kreis um Bruno Taut 1919–1920*, Kat. Museum Schloß Morsbroich, Leverkusen, Akademie der Künste, Berlin 1963.

Morphologie – City Metaphors, Cologne 1982.

Architettura come tema – Architecture as theme, Die Thematisierung der Architektur, Milan 1982, Stuttgart 1983.

Sieben Variationen des Raumes über die Sieben Leuchter der Baukunst von John Ruskin, Stuttgart, Cologne 1985.

O. M. Ungers 1951–1984, Bauten und Projekte, ed. Heinrich Klotz, Braunschweig, Wiesbaden 1985.

Quadratische Häuser, Stuttgart 1986.

Oswald Mathias Ungers. Architektur 1951–1990, Stuttgart 1991 – *Architetture 1951–1990*, Milan 1991 (detailed bibliography).

O. M. Ungers – Architekt, cat. Hamburger Kunsthalle, Hamburg 1994.

Oswald Mathias Ungers, Bauten und Projekte 1991 to 1998, Stuttgart 1998.

... and Stefan Vieths, *Die dialektische Stadt*, Braunschweig, Wiesbaden, Cologne 1999.

Aphorismen zum Häuserbauen, Cologne 1999.

10 Kapitel über Architektur. Ein visueller Traktat, Cologne 1999.

»Oswald Mathias Ungers. Berliner Vorlesungen 1964/1965«, *arch+* (July 2006), 179.

»Lernen von O. M. Ungers. Die Berliner Lehrzeit 1963 to 1969«, ed. Erika Mühlthaler, *archplus* (Dec. 2006), 181/182.

Literatur über Oswald Mathias Ungers (Auswahl)
Literature about Oswald Mathias Ungers (selection)

»Architektur in Deutschland«, in: *Das Kunstwerk*, (1979), 2–3, pp. 132–141.

Aymonino, Carlo, »Il contributo di Oswald Mathias Ungers all'architettura«, in: *Controspazio*, 3 (1975), pp. 2–43.

Banham, Reyner, *Brutalismus in der Architektur*. *Ethik oder Ästhetik?*, Stuttgart 1966, pp. 125 f., 144 f.

Bisogli, L., »Germania di oggi: O. M. Ungers«, in: *Casabella*, 305 (1966), pp. 36–59.

Brown-Manrique, Gerardo, *O. M. Ungers. A Comprehensive Bibliography 1953 to 1995,* Oxford/Ohio 1996.

Cepl, Jasper, »Ungers und seine Bücher, Die Bibliothek als Sammlung der Ideen«, in: Lepik 2006, pp. 30–40.

Cepl, Jasper, *Oswald Mathias Ungers. Eine intellektuelle Biographie.* Cologne 2007.

Cepl, Jasper, »Das Haus im Haus, die Puppe in der Puppe – und die Entwurfsidee in der Entwurfsidee?«, in: Winkelmann 2008, pp. 13–34.

Conrads, Ulrich; Werner Marschall, *Neue deutsche Architektur 2, New German Architecture 2*, Stuttgart 1962, pp. 39–41, 44.

Dammann, Klaus, *Architektenhäuser der Gegenwartsarchitektur in Deutschland,* Magisterarbeit Universität Tübingen, Tübingen 1987.

Elser, Oliver, *Die Sammlung der Architekturmodelle nach eigenen oder historischen Entwürfen*, in: Lepik 2006, pp. 41–53.

»Ein Werkstattbericht – Bauten und Projekte von O. M. Ungers«, in: *Bauwelt*, 8, 1960, pp. 204–217.

Finanzministerium Baden-Württemberg (ed.), *Die Badische Landesbibliothek Karlsruhe*, Stuttgart 1992.

Foos, Peter, *Möbel als Metapher*, Cologne 2012.

Fußbroich, Helmut, *Architekturführer Köln. Profane Architektur nach 1900*, Cologne 1997.

Giedion, Sigfried, *Time, Space, Architecture*, 1941 ff.; dt.: *Raum, Zeit, Architektur*, Ravensburg 1965.

Gierschner, Sabina, »Das Buch und sein Haus – Der Bibliothekskubus von O. M. Ungers in Köln-Müngersdorf«, in: *in situ* (2012) 1, pp. 131–141.

Gieselmann, Reinhard, Oswald Mathias Ungers (1960), »Zu einer neuen Architektur«, in: *Der Monat*, 174 (March 1963) and in: Ulrich Conrads (ed.), *Programme und Manifeste zur Architektur des 20. Jahrhundert. Bauwelt Fundamente*, 1, Berlin 1964, pp. 158 f.

Gieselmann, Reinhard, »OMU's Ecke 1959 und 1989«, in: Sieber-Albers, Kieren 1999, pp. 50–52.

Gieselmann, Reinhard. On the Search of Style. Auf der Suche nach Stil, with an essay by Gerhard Kabierske, Stuttgart 2007.

Jürgensen, Klaus, »Das Haus des Architekten«, in: *Deutsche Bauzeitung*, 126 (1992), 9, pp. 100–102.

Kierdorf, Alexander, *Köln. Ein Architekturführer,* Berlin 1999.

Kieren, Martin, *Oswald Mathias Ungers*, Zurich, Munich, London 1994.

Kieren, Martin, »Der Architekt als Bauherr, Ungers' eigene Häuser als Ergebnis einer monologischen Kunst«, in: Lepik 2006, pp. 55–67.

Kieren, Martin, »O. M. Ungers«, in: Liselotte Ungers, Über *Architekten. Leben, Werk & Theorie*, Cologne 2002, pp. 341–359.

Klotz, Heinrich, *Architektur in der Bundesrepublik. Gespräche mit sechs Architekten. Günter Behnisch, Wolfgang Döring, Helmut Hentrich, Hans Kammerer, Frei Otto, Oswald Mathias Ungers*, Berlin 1977, pp. 98–113.

Klotz, Heinrich, »›Die Berliner Schule‹ 1963–1967, Oswald Mathias Ungers als Lehrer«, in: Deutsches Architekturmuseum Frankfurt (ed.)., Braunschweig, Wiesbaden 1981, pp. 123–130.

Klotz, Heinrich, *Moderne und Postmoderne. Architektur der Gegenwart 1960–1980.* Braunschweig, Wiesbaden 1984, pp. 214–234.

Klotz, Heinrich (ed.), *Die Revision der Moderne. Postmoderne Architektur 1960–1980*, Munich 1984, pp. 297 to 321.

Klotz, Heinrich, *Weitergegeben. Erinnerungen*, Cologne 1999, pp. 203–207.

Koenig, Giovanni Klaus, *Architettura Tedesca del Secondo Dopoguerra*, Bologna 1965.

Lepik, Andres (ed.), *O. M. Ungers, Kosmos der Architektur*, Kat. Nationalgalerie Staatliche Museen Berlin, Ostfildern 2006.

Magnago Lampugnani, Vittorio, »Die Geste und ihr Schatten. Anmerkungen zum Gebäude des Deutschen Architekturmuseums in Frankfurt am Main«, in: *Deutsches Architekturmuseum Frankfurt am Main. Festschrift zur Eröffnung am 1. Juni 1984*, pp. 27–37.

Mainzer, Udo, »Oswald Mathias Ungers – Denkmal-Architekt im Rheinland«, in: *Denkmalpflege im Rheinland*, 28 (2011), 2, pp. 49–60.

Mühlthaler, Erika (ed.), »Lernen von O. M. Ungers«, in: *archplus*, 181/182 (December 2006).

Nestler, Paolo, Peter M. Bode, *Deutsche Kunst seit 1960. Architektur*, Munich 1976, p. 39.

Neumeyer, Fritz, »Die Stadt in der Stadt oder: Der Architekt als Hermeneutiker des Urbanen«, in: *O. M. Ungers, Architekturmodelle und -Zeichnungen,* cat. Kulturforum Alte Post Neuss, 1991.

Neumeyer, Fritz, »Architektonisches Enigma. Ein Ganzes für sich und eine Einheit aus Einzelheiten«, in: Ungers 1991, pp. 7–23.

Pehnt, Wolfgang, *Neue Deutsche Architektur 3*, Stuttgart 1970, pp. 30, 33, 56 f., 86–89.

Pehnt, Wolfgang, »Am alltäglichen Ort«, in: *Frankfurter Allgemeine Zeitung*, 15 May 1981, also in: Schreiber (ed.) 1986, pp. 47–49.

Pehnt, Wolfgang, »Die Kaaba von Müngersdorf«, in: *Frankfurter Allgemeine Zeitung*, 10 January 1991.

Pehnt, Wolfgang, »Nutrimentum spiritus. Die Badische Landesbibliothek«, in: Sieber-Albers, Kieren 1999, pp. 126–132.

Pehnt, Wolfgang, *Deutsche Architektur seit 1900*, Munich 2005.

Pehnt, Wolfgang, »Bild und Bilderverbot. Rudolf Schwarz und Oswald Mathias Ungers: zwei Kölner Nachbarn«, in: *Rudolf Schwarz und seine Zeitgenossen*, Cologne 2011, pp. 169–186.

Pevsner, Nikolaus, »Moderne Architektur und der Historiker, oder Die Wiederkehr des Historizismus«, in: *Deutsche Bauzeitung*, 66 (1961) 10, pp. 757–764, and: »Wiederkehr des Historismus«, in: *Architektur und Design. Von der Romantik zur Sachlichkeit*, Munich 1971, pp. 489–509.

»Protagonista dell'architettura contemporanea (1) O. M. Ungers«, in: *Rassegna Dell'Istituto di Architettura e Urbanistica*, Rome 1965, pp. 64–97.

Rossi, Aldo, »Un giovane architetto tedesco: Oswald Mathias Ungers«, in: *Casabella*, 244 (1960), pp. 22–35.

Sawade, Jürgen, »Wohnhaus Ungers 3, in Köln-Müngersdorf«, in: Sieber-Albers, Kieren 1999, pp. 140 to 143.

Schreiber, Mathias (ed.). *Deutsche Architektur nach 1945*, Stuttgart 1986, pp. 47–49.

Schwarz, Hans-Peter (ed.), *Künstlerhäuser. Eine Architekturgeschichte des Privaten,* Kat. Deutsches Architektur-Museum Frankfurt am Main, Braunschweig 1989.

Schwarz, Hans-Peter, *Das Künstlerhaus. Anmerkungen zur Sozialgeschichte des Genies*, Braunschweig 1990.

Sieber-Albers, Anja; Martin Kieren (ed.), *Sichtweisen. Betrachtungen zum Werk von O. M. Ungers*, Braunschweig, Wiesbaden, Cologne 1999.

Stabenow, Jörg, »Weihestätte und Bekenntnisbau – der Durchbruch zur Moderne im Spiegel des Künstlerhauses«, in: Hans-Peter Schwarz (ed.) 1989, pp. 80–163.

Stabenow, Jörg, *Architekten wohnen. Ihre Domizile im 20. Jahrhundert*, Berlin, 2000, especially: »Selbstkritik der Moderne, Oswald Mathias Ungers«, pp. 188–205.

Strodthoff, Werner, »Eine Privatbibliothek in Köln-Müngersdorf«, in: *Bauwelt*, 82 (1991), 16, pp. 830–833.

Tasch, Stephanie, »Ein Besuch im Haus des Architekten. Die Kunstsammlung Oswald Mathias Ungers«, in: Lepik 2006, pp. 19–29.

Ungers Archiv für Architekturwissenschaft (ed.), *O. M. Ungers. Kosmos der Architektur*, preface by Martin Kieren, Cologne 2006.

Winkelmann, Arne (ed.), *Das Haus im Haus. Zur Wirkungsgeschichte einer Entwurfsidee*, Heidelberg 2008.

Biographie

1926 geboren in Kaisersesch, Eifel
1947 Abitur in Mayen, Eifel
1947–1950 Studium der Architektur an der TH Karlsruhe, Diplom bei Egon Eiermann
1950–1955 Architekturbüro in Partnerschaft mit Helmut Goldschmidt
1955 eigenes Büro in Köln
1956 Heirat mit Liselotte Gabler
1963–1969 Professor für Entwerfen und Gebäudekunde an der TU Berlin
1965, 1967 Visiting Critic an der Cornell University, Ithaca, NY
1969–1976 Professor für Architektur an der Cornell University, Ithaca, NY
1973, 1978 Professor für Architektur an der Harvard University, Cambridge, Mass.
1974, 1975 Professor für Architektur an der University of California, Los Angeles, Calif.
1979, 1980 Professor für Architektur an der Hochschule für Angewandte Kunst Wien
1986–1990 Professor für Architektur an der Kunstakademie Düsseldorf
1987 Großer BDA-Preis des Bundes Deutscher Architekten
1999 Dr.-Ing. h. c. der TU Berlin
2000 Großer DAI Preis für Baukultur des Verbandes Deutscher Architekten- und Ingenieurvereine
2000 Mitglied der Akademie der Künste, Berlin
2007 gestorben in Köln

Biography

1926 born in Kaisersesch, Eifel
1947 *Abitur* in Mayen, Eifel
1947–1950 studied architecture at the TH Karlsruhe, diploma with Egon Eiermann
1950–1955 architectural office in partnership with Helmut Goldschmidt
1955 own office in Cologne
1956 marriage with Liselotte Gabler
1963–1969 professor of design and building typology at the TU Berlin
1965, 1967 visiting critic at Cornell University, Ithaca, NY
1969–1976 professor of architecture at Cornell University, Ithaca, NY
1973, 1978 professor of architecture at Harvard University, Cambridge, Mass.
1974, 1975 professor of architecture at the University of California, Los Angeles, Calif.
1979, 1980 professor of architecture at the Hochschule für Angewandte Kunst Wien
1986–1990 professor of architecture at the Kunstakademie Düsseldorf
1987 Großer BDA-Preis of the Bund Deutscher Architekten
1999 Dr.-Ing. h. c. of the TU Berlin
2000 Großer DAI Preis für Baukultur of the Verband Deutscher Architekten- und Ingenieurvereine
2000 member of the Akademie der Künste, Berlin
2007 died in Cologne

1, 2. Ideenskizzen von Oswald Mathias Ungers, um 1958.

1, 2. Conceptual sketches by Oswald Mathias Ungers, c. 1958.

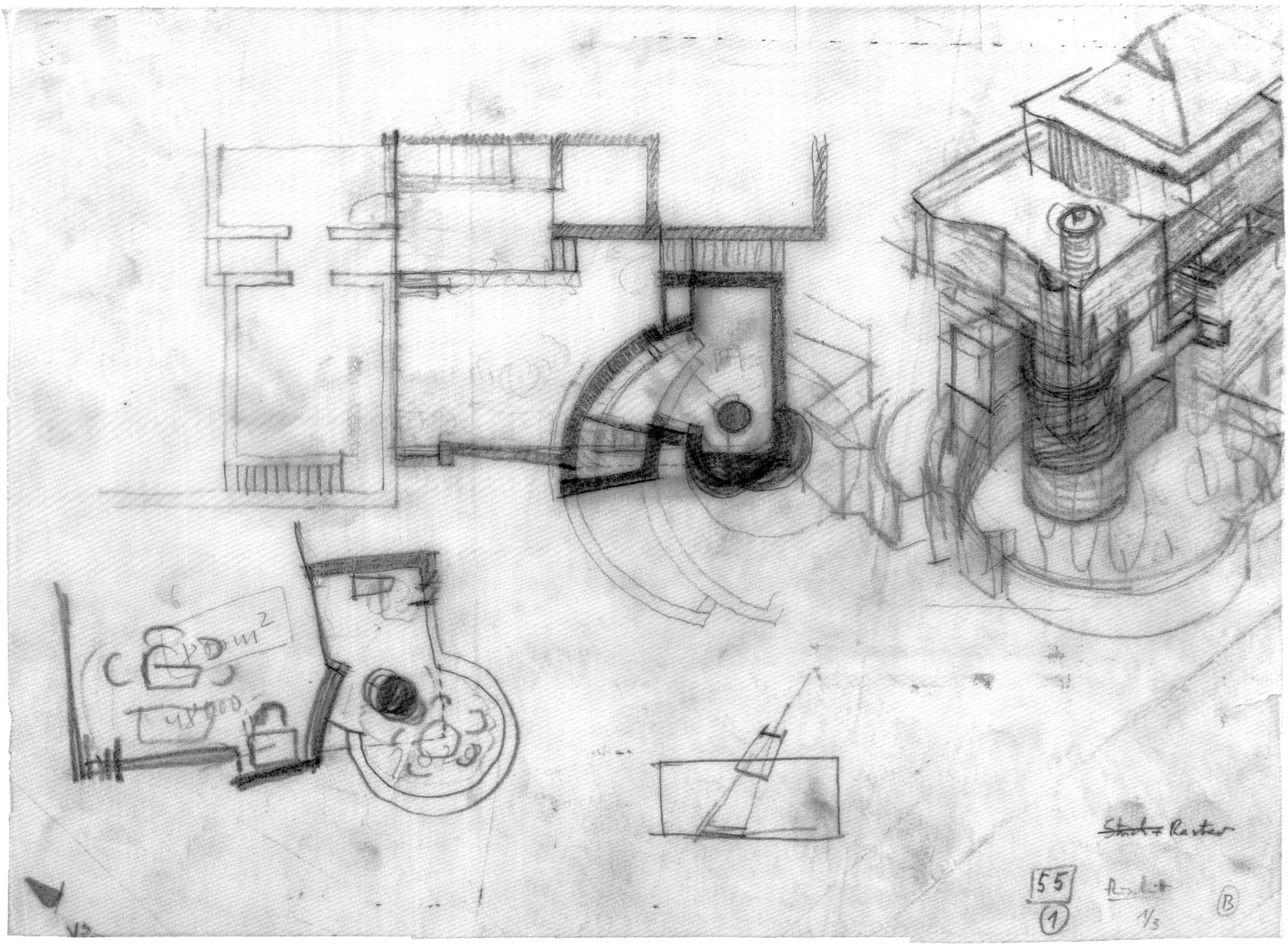

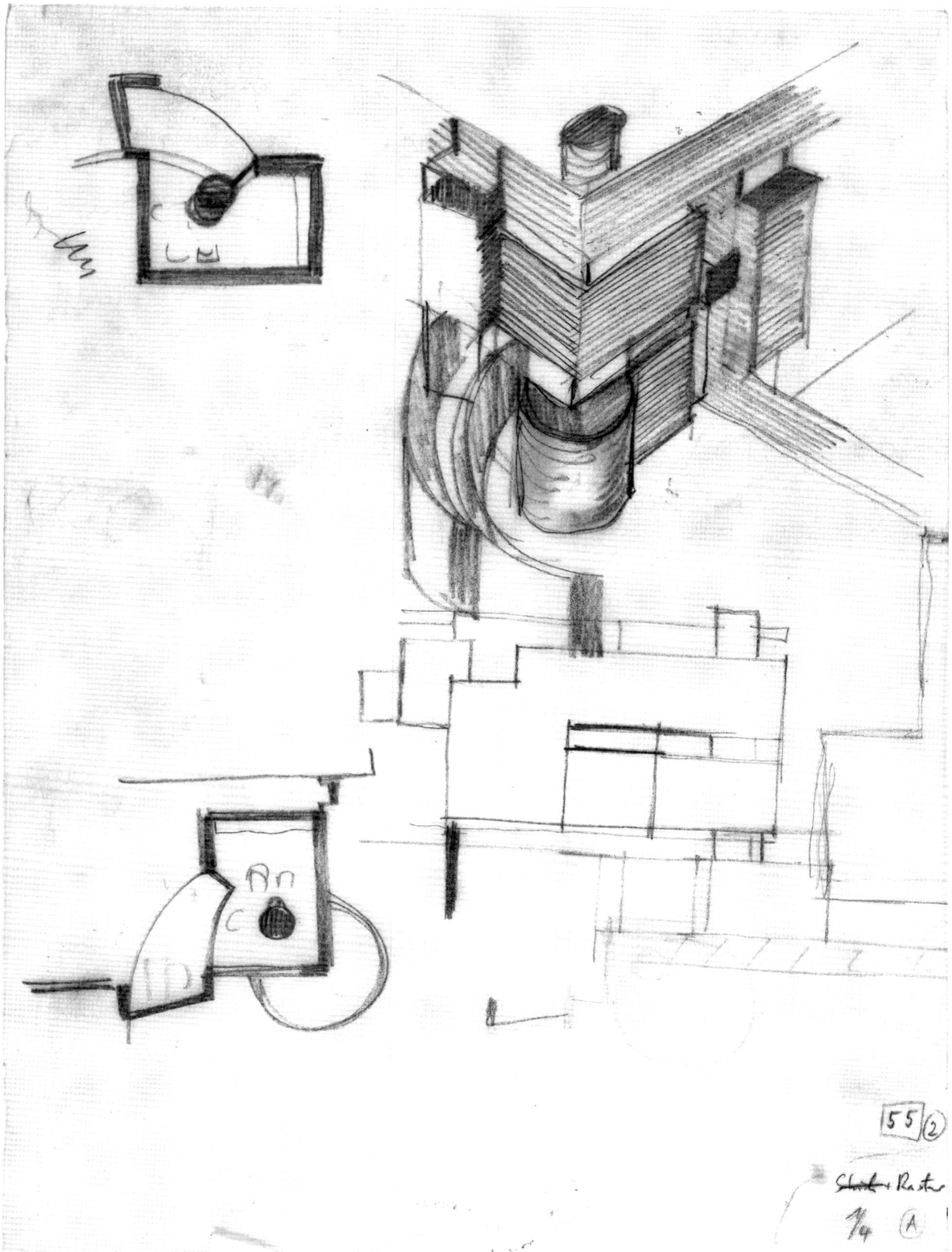

3. Grundriß (Erdgeschoß) der Baustufe von 1958/59.

S. 34, 35
4, 5. Grundrisse (Obergeschoß und Dachgeschoß) der Baustufe von 1958/59.

3. Floor plan (ground floor) of the construction stage of 1958/59.

pp. 34, 35
4, 5. Floor plans (upper floor and attic floor) of the 1958/59 construction stage.

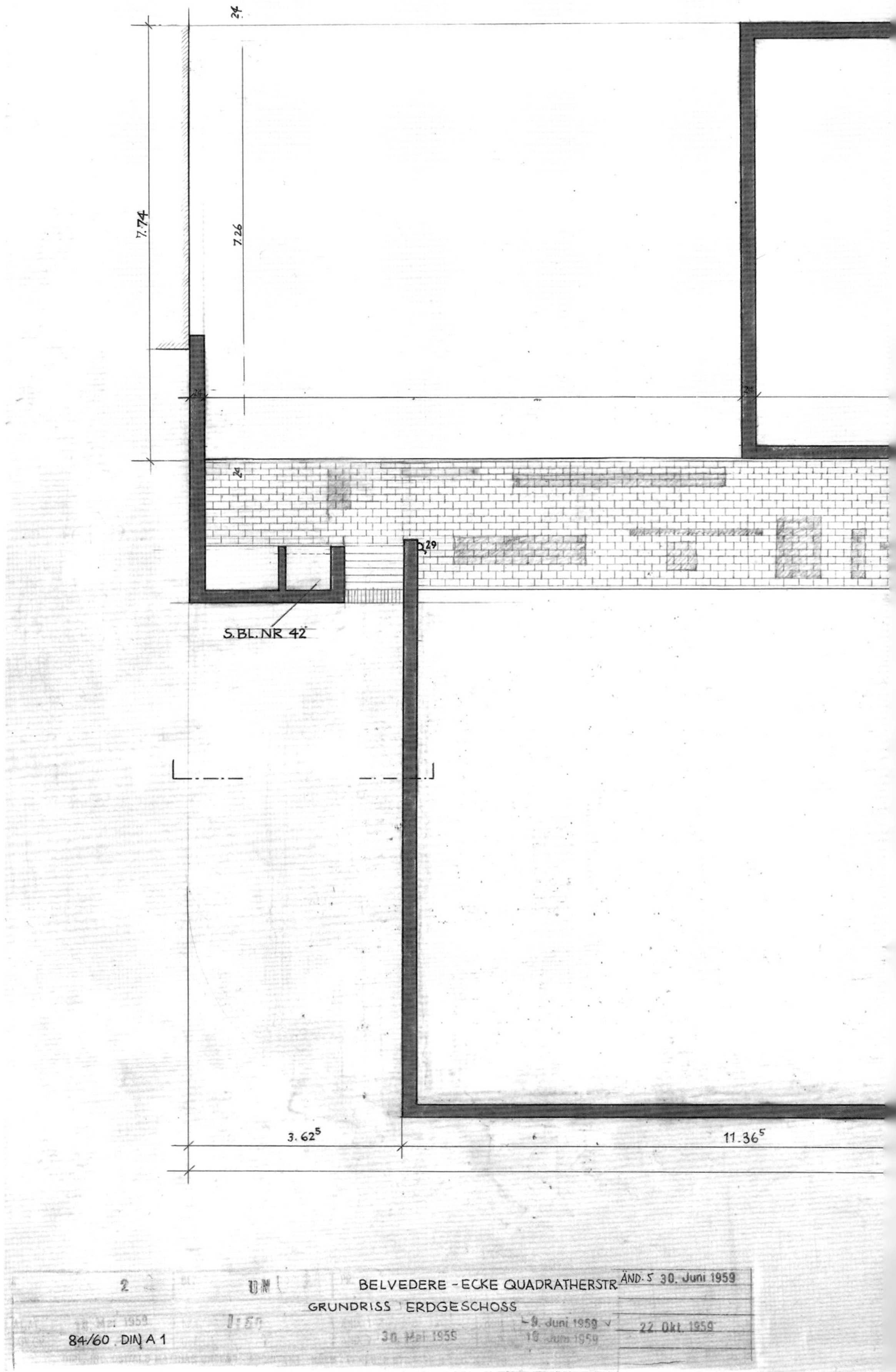

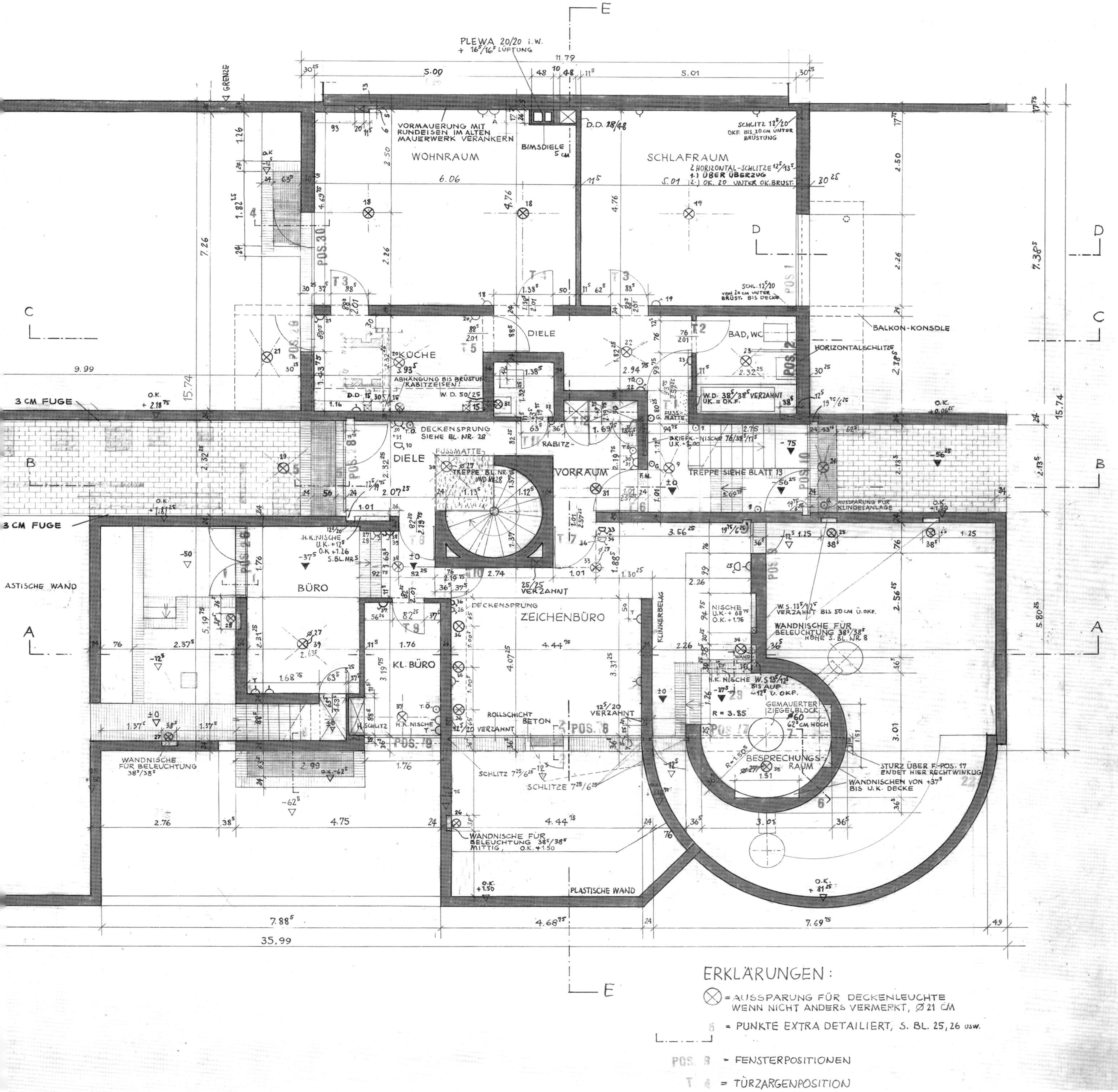

PLEWA 20/20 i.W.
GRENZE
WOHNRAUM
SCHLAFRAUM
VORMAUERUNG MIT RUNDEISEN IM ALTEN MAUERWERK VERANKERN
BIMSDIELE
KÜCHE
DIELE
BAD, WC
BALKON-KONSOLE
HORIZONTALSCHLITZE
3 CM FUGE
VORRAUM
TREPPE SIEHE BLATT 13
BÜRO
KL. BÜRO
ZEICHENBÜRO
BESPRECHUNGS-RAUM
KLINKERBELAG
PLASTISCHE WAND
ROLLSCHICHT BETON
GEMAUERTER ZIEGELBLOCK
STURZ ÜBER F.-POS. 17 ENDET HIER RECHTWINKLIG
WANDNISCHEN VON +37⁵ BIS U.K. DECKE
WANDNISCHE FÜR BELEUCHTUNG
35.99
ERKLÄRUNGEN:
= AUSSPARUNG FÜR DECKENLEUCHTE WENN NICHT ANDERS VERMERKT, Ø 21 CM
= PUNKTE EXTRA DETAILIERT, S. BL. 25, 26 usw.
POS. 8 = FENSTERPOSITIONEN
T 4 = TÜRZARGENPOSITION

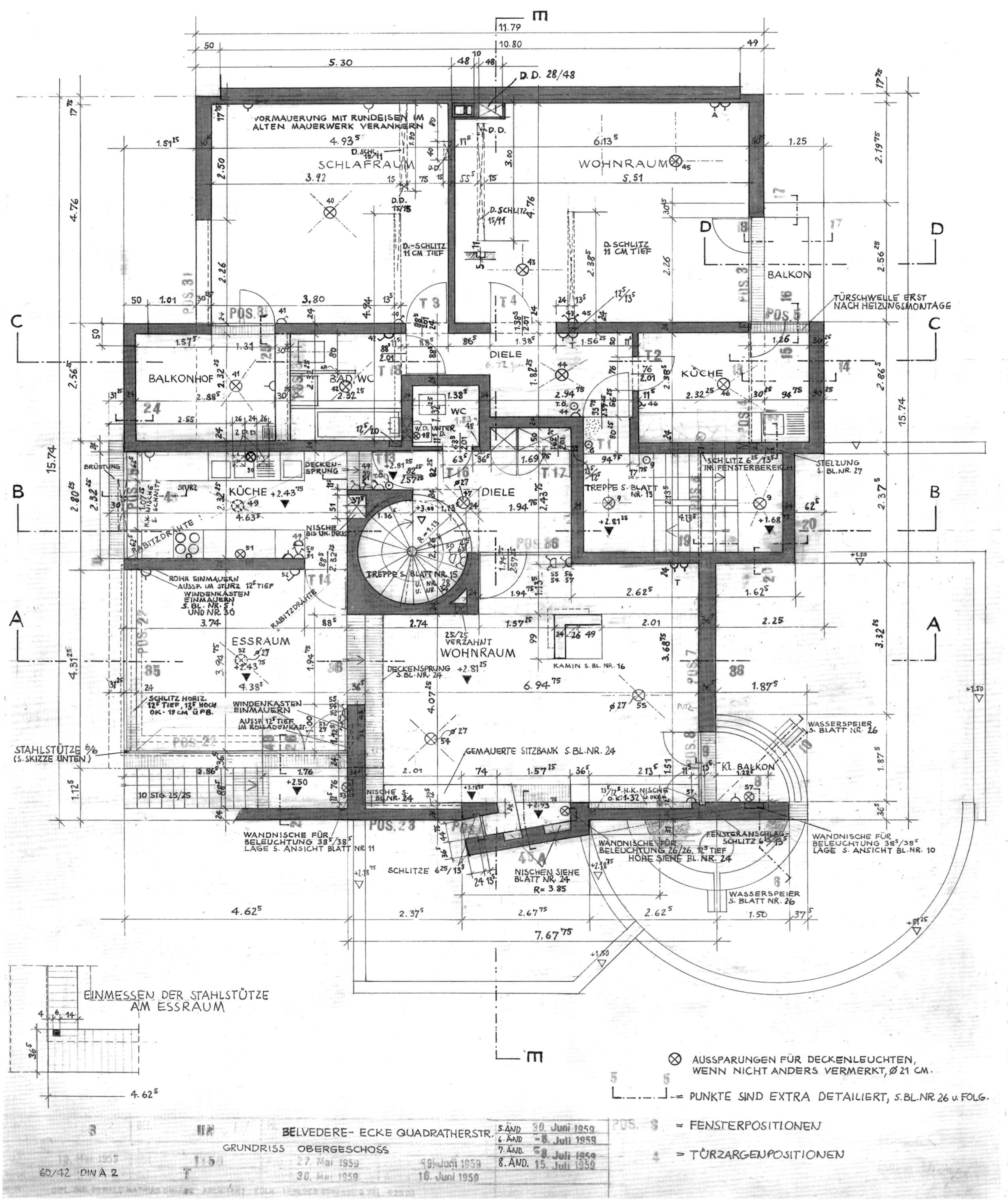

BELVEDERE- ECKE QUADRATHERSTR.
GRUNDRISS OBERGESCHOSS
SCHLAFRAUM
WOHNRAUM
BALKON
BALKONHOF
BAD, WC
DIELE
KÜCHE
WC
ESSRAUM
TREPPE S. BLATT NR. 15
KL. BALKON
EINMESSEN DER STAHLSTÜTZE AM ESSRAUM
AUSSPARUNGEN FÜR DECKENLEUCHTEN, WENN NICHT ANDERS VERMERKT, Ø 21 CM.
= PUNKTE SIND EXTRA DETAILIERT, S.BL.NR. 26 u. FOLG.
= FENSTERPOSITIONEN
= TÜRZARGENPOSITIONEN

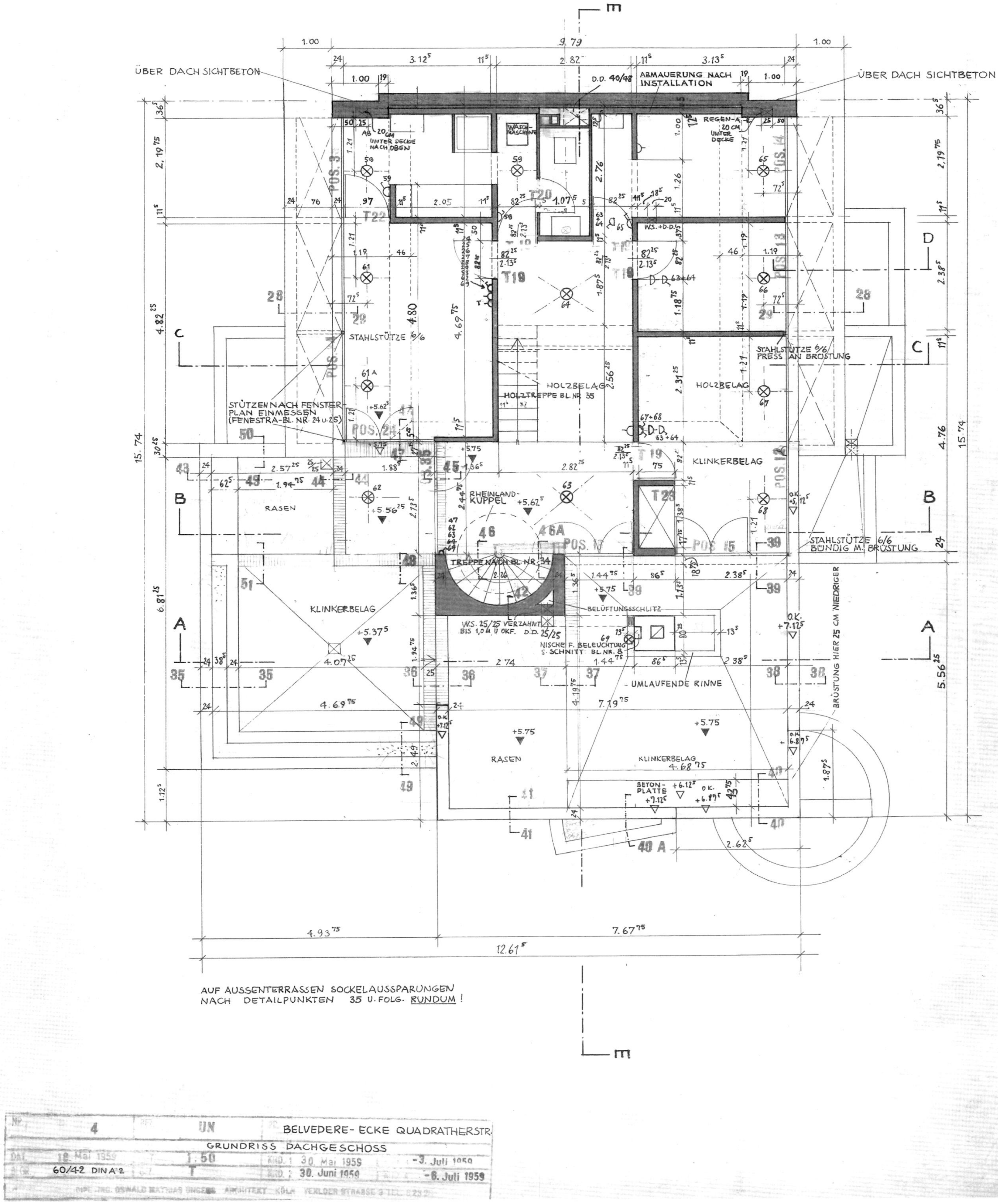

ÜBER DACH SICHTBETON
ABMAUERUNG NACH INSTALLATION
ÜBER DACH SICHTBETON
STAHLSTÜTZE 6/6
STÜTZEN NACH FENSTER PLAN EINMESSEN (FENESTRA-BL. NR. 24 u. 25)
HOLZBELAG
HOLZTREPPE BL. NR. 35
STAHLSTÜTZE 6/6 PRESS AN BRÜSTUNG
KLINKERBELAG
RASEN
RHEINLAND-KUPPEL
STAHLSTÜTZE 6/6 BÜNDIG M. BRÜSTUNG
TREPPE NACH BL. NR. 34
BELÜFTUNGSSCHLITZ
NISCHE F. BELEUCHTUNG S. SCHNITT BL. NR. 8
UMLAUFENDE RINNE
BRÜSTUNG HIER 25 CM NIEDRIGER
BETON-PLATTE
AUF AUSSENTERRASSEN SOCKELAUSSPARUNGEN NACH DETAILPUNKTEN 35 U. FOLG. RUNDUM!
BELVEDERE-ECKE QUADRATHERSTR.
GRUNDRISS DACHGESCHOSS
1:50
60/4-2 DIN A 2
30. Juni 1959
-6. Juli 1959

6. Gesamtansicht von Norden, 1960. (Photo: Walter Ehmann.)
7. Gesamtansicht von Westen, 1960. (Photo: Walter Ehmann.)

6. General view from the north, 1960. (Photo: Walter Ehmann.)
7. General view from the west, 1960. (Photo: Walter Ehmann.)

8. Zeichenraum im Erdgeschoß, 1960. (Photo: Walter Ehmann.)
9. Besprechungsraum im Erdgeschoß, 1960. (Photo: Walter Ehmann.)
10. Ursprüngliche Bibliothek in der ehemaligen Einliegerwohnung im Obergeschoß mit Liselotte und Oswald Mathias Ungers, 1982. (Photo: Dr. Frickinger.)

8. Drawing room on the ground floor, 1960. (Photo: Walter Ehmann.)
9. Conference room on the ground floor, 1960. (Photo: Walter Ehmann.)
10. Original library in the former granny-flat on the upper floor with Liselotte and Oswald Mathias Ungers, 1982. (Photo: Dr. Frickinger.)

11. Diele mit Durchblick zum Wohnraum im Obergeschoß, 1960. (Photo: Walter Ehmann.)
12. Wohnraum im Obergeschoß, 1960. (Photo: Walter Ehmann.)

11. Vestibule with view toward the living room on the upper floor, 1960. (Photo: Walter Ehmann.)
12. Living room on the upper floor, 1960. (Photo: Walter Ehmann.)

13. Vorraum zu den Schlafräumen mit Zugang zu der Dachterrasse im Dachgeschoß, 1960. (Photo: Walter Ehmann.)
14. Dachterrasse im Dachgeschoß, 1960. (Photo: Walter Ehmann.)

S. 44, 45
15–18. Grundrisse (Kellergeschoß, Erdgeschoß, Obergeschoß, Dachgeschoß) der Baustufe von 1989/90.

S. 46, 47
19–22. Grundrisse (Kellergeschoß, Erdgeschoß, Obergeschoß, Dachgeschoß) mit Überlagerung der Baustufen von 1958/59 und 1989/90, erarbeitet und gezeichnet von Bernd Grimm.

13. Anteroom to the bedrooms with access to the roof terrace on the attic floor, 1960. (Photo: Walter Ehmann.)
14. Roof terrace on the attic floor, 1960. (Photo: Walter Ehmann.)

pp. 44, 45
15–18. Floor plans (basement floor, ground floor, upper-floor, attic floor) of the 1989/90 construction stage.

pp. 46, 47
19–22. Floor plans (basement floor, ground floor, upper floor, attic floor) with overlay of the 1958/59 and the 1989/90 construction stages, worked out and drawn by Bernd Grimm.

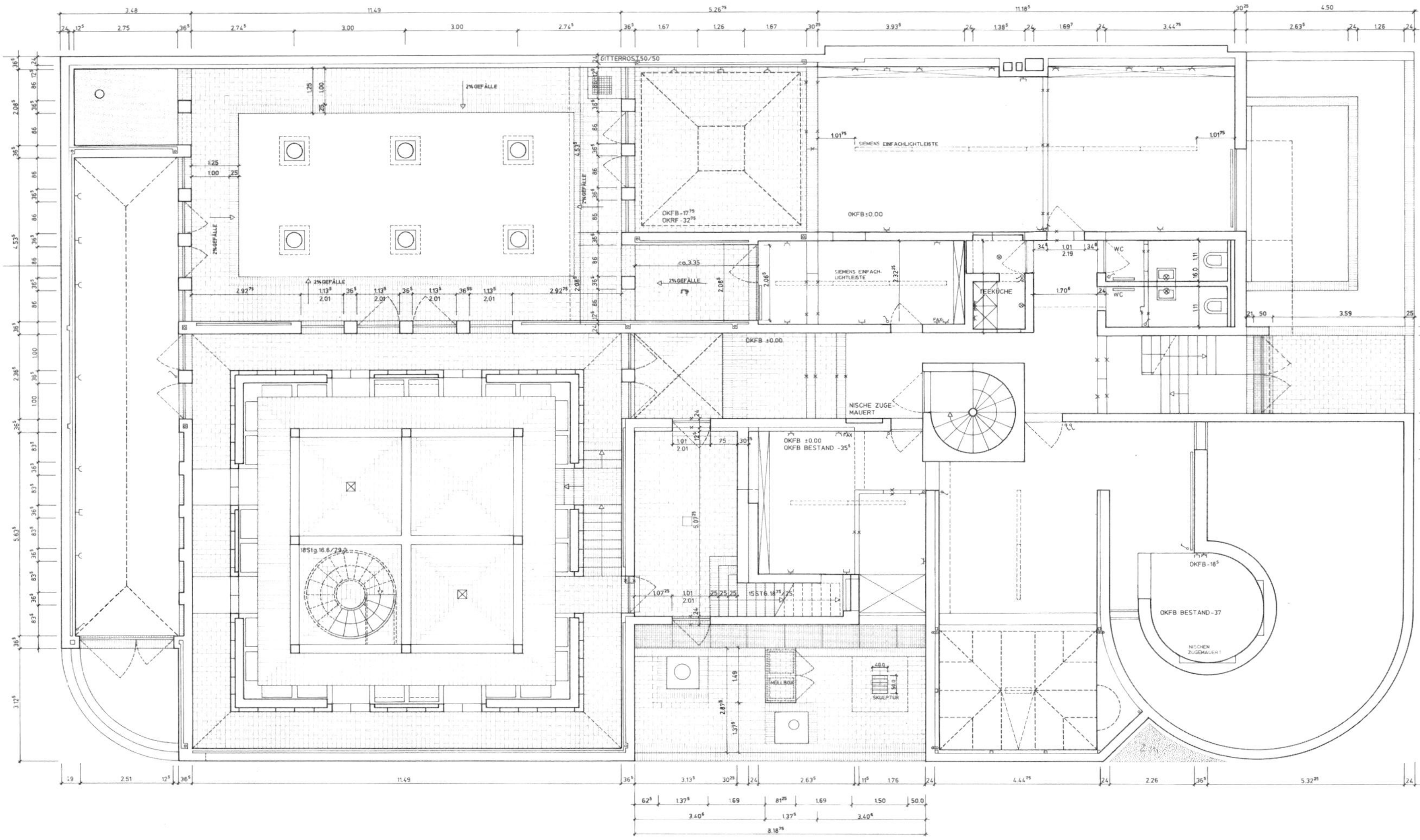

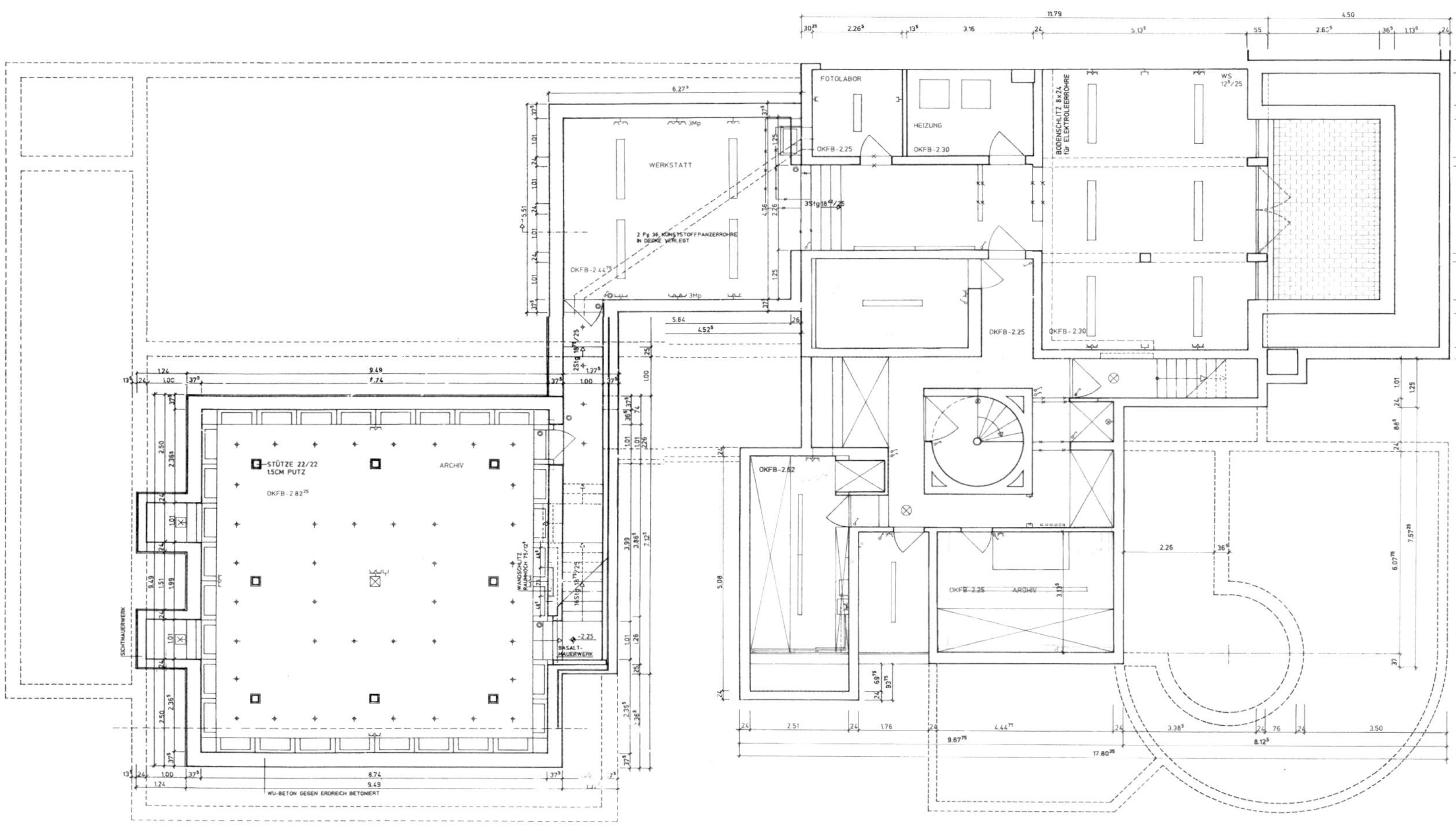
FOTOLABOR
HEIZUNG
WERKSTATT
ARCHIV

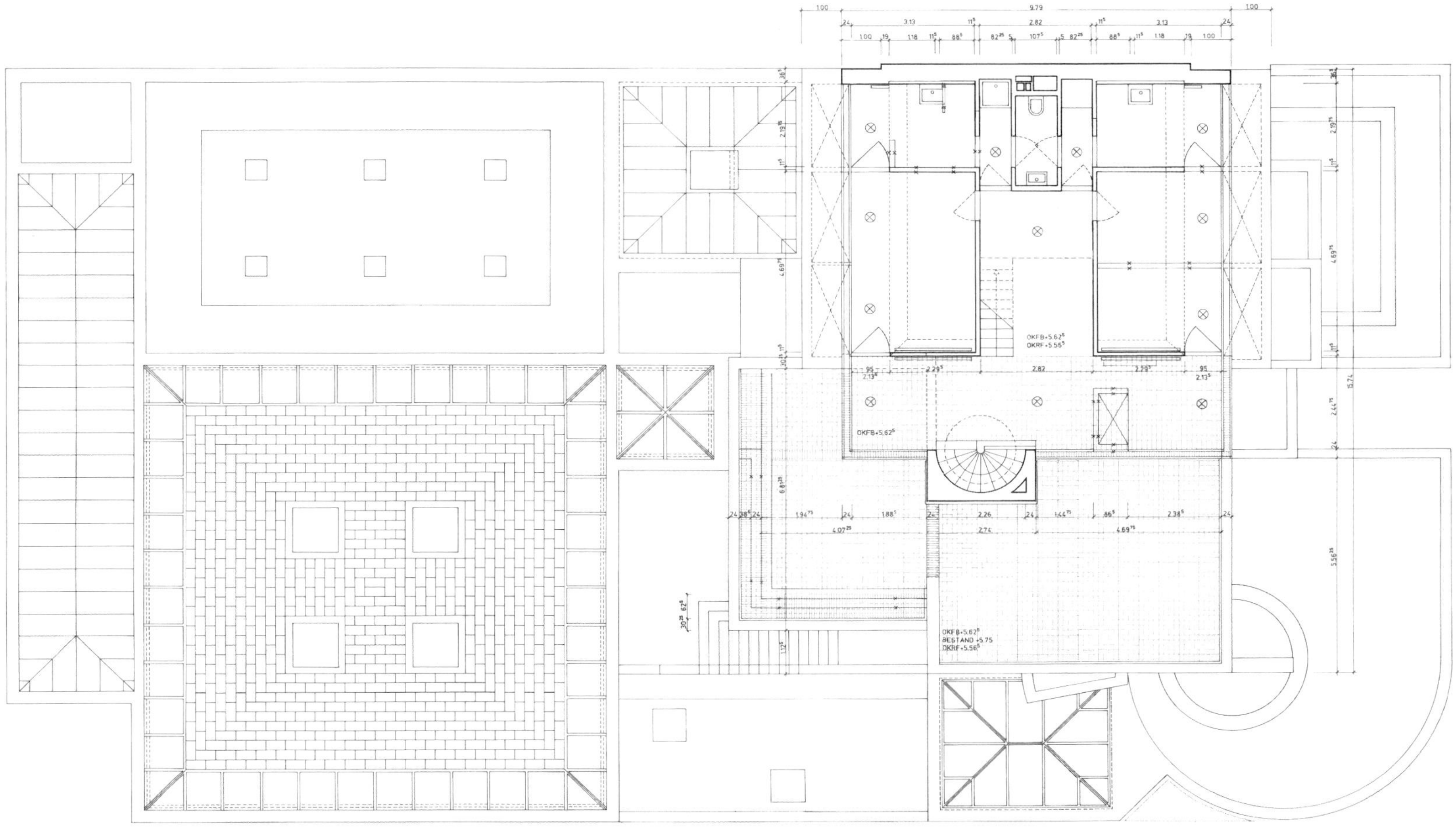

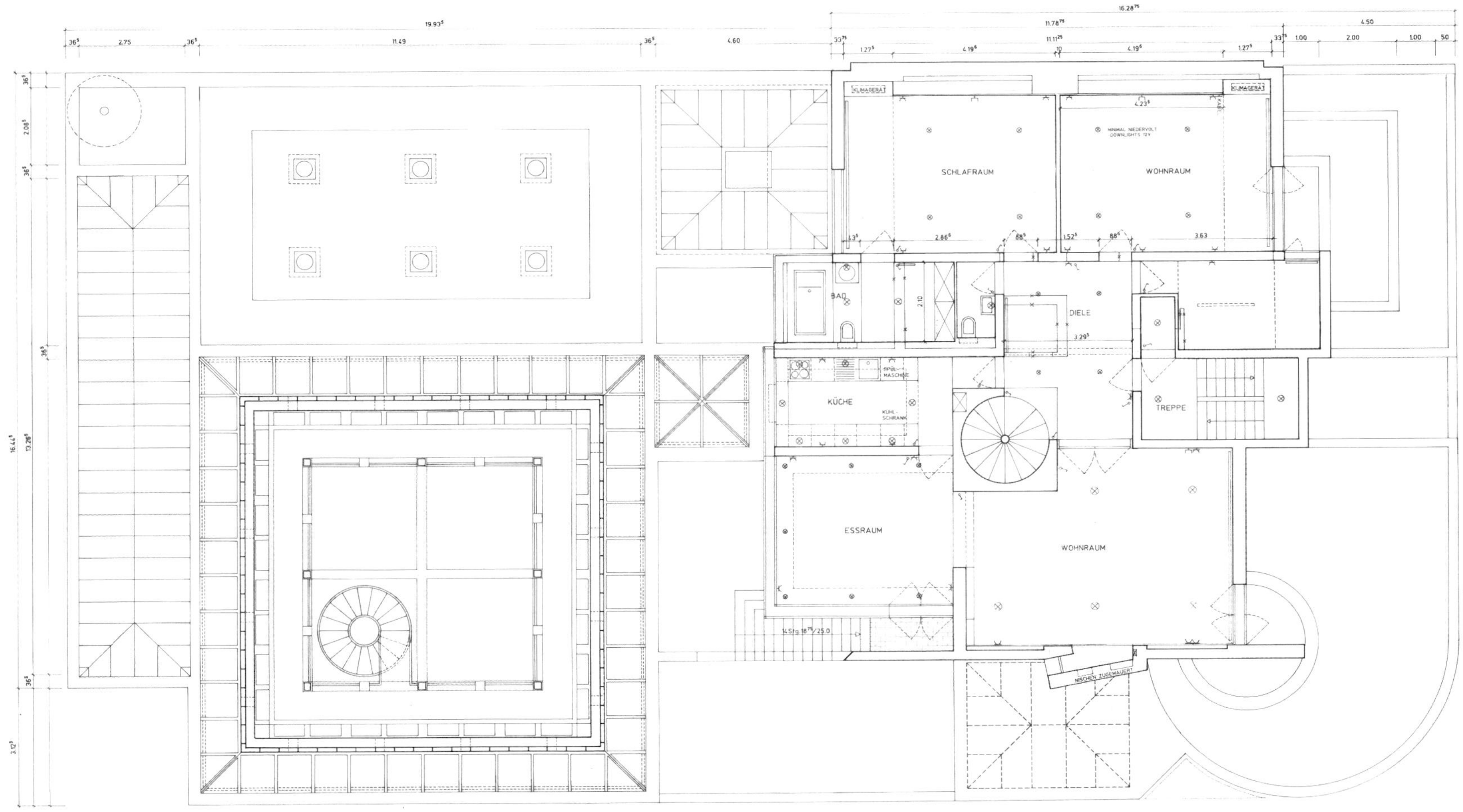
SCHLAFRAUM
WOHNRAUM
BAD
DIELE
KÜCHE
TREPPE
ESSRAUM
WOHNRAUM

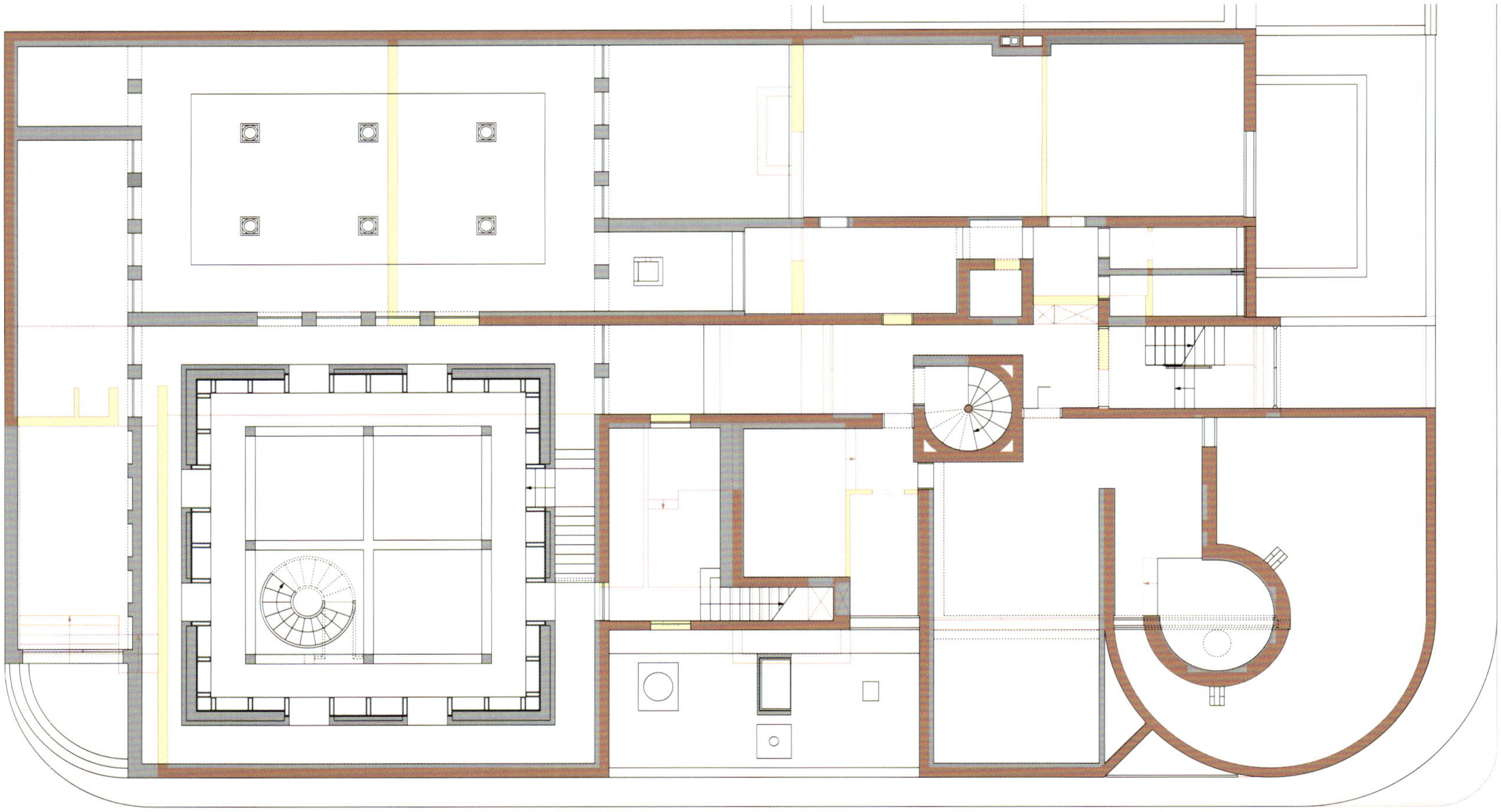

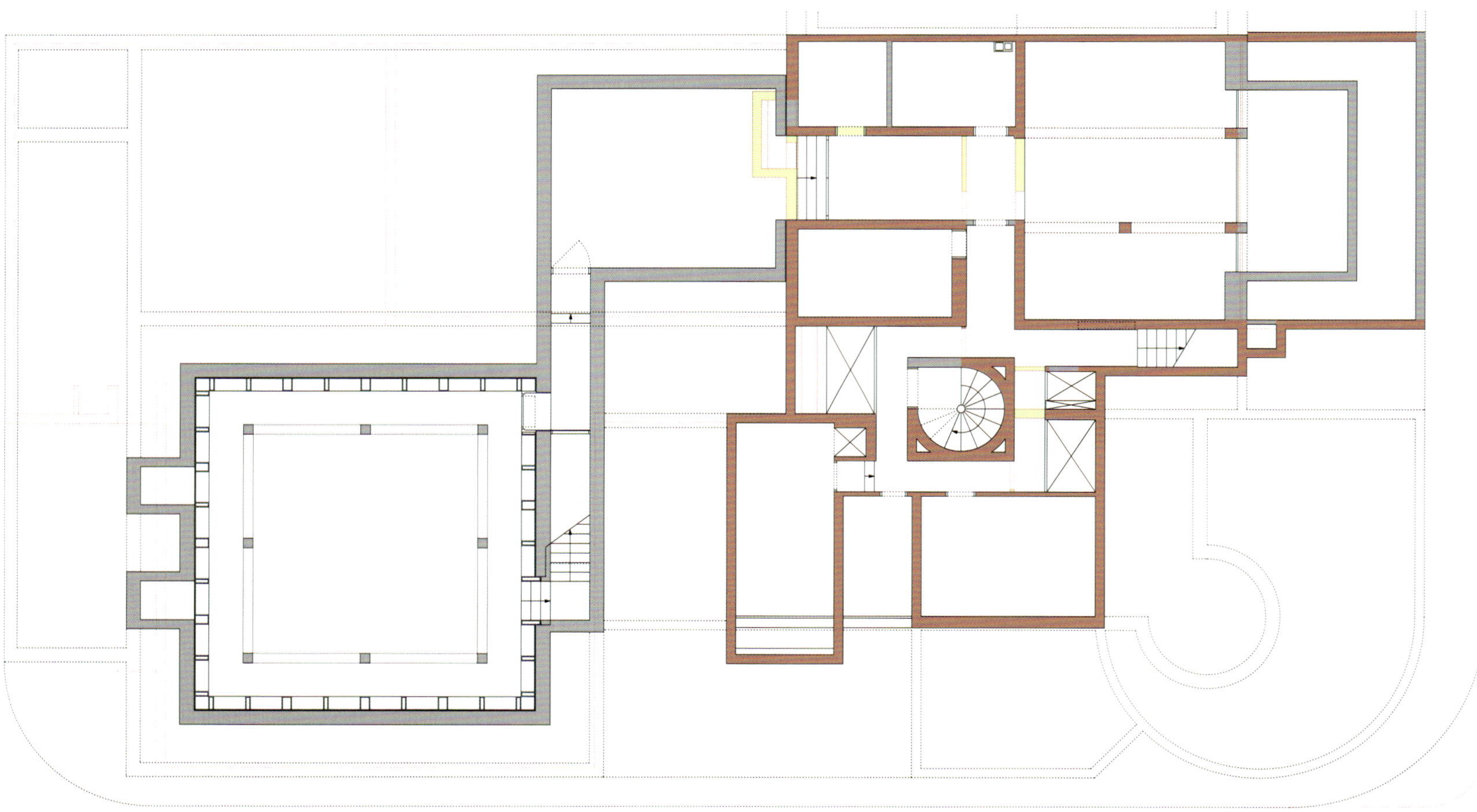

Bauzustand 1959
Abriss 1989/1990
Bauzustand 1990

M 1:100 0 1 2 3 4 5 6 7 8 9 10 11 12 13 14 15 16 17 18 19 20 Meter

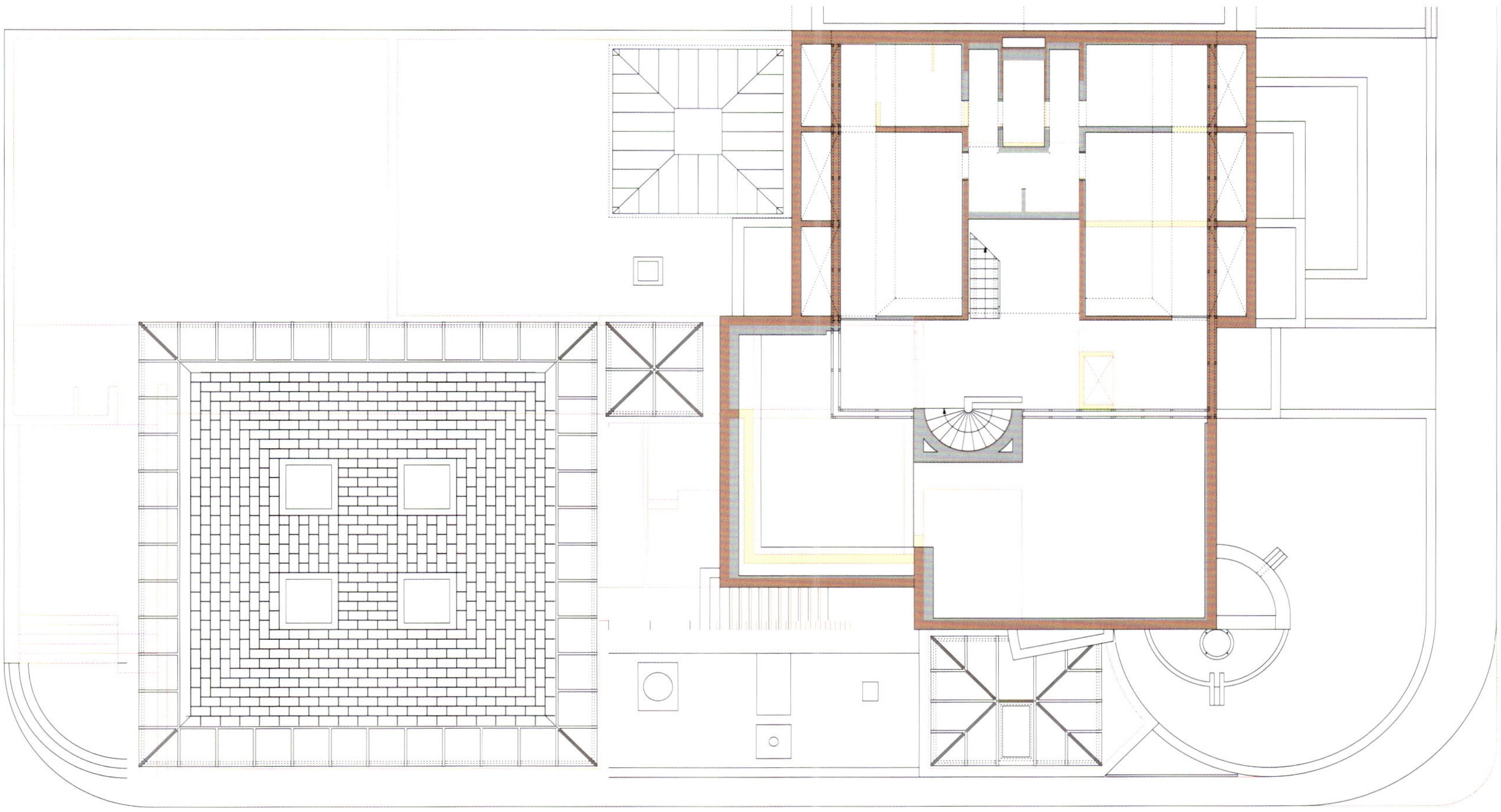

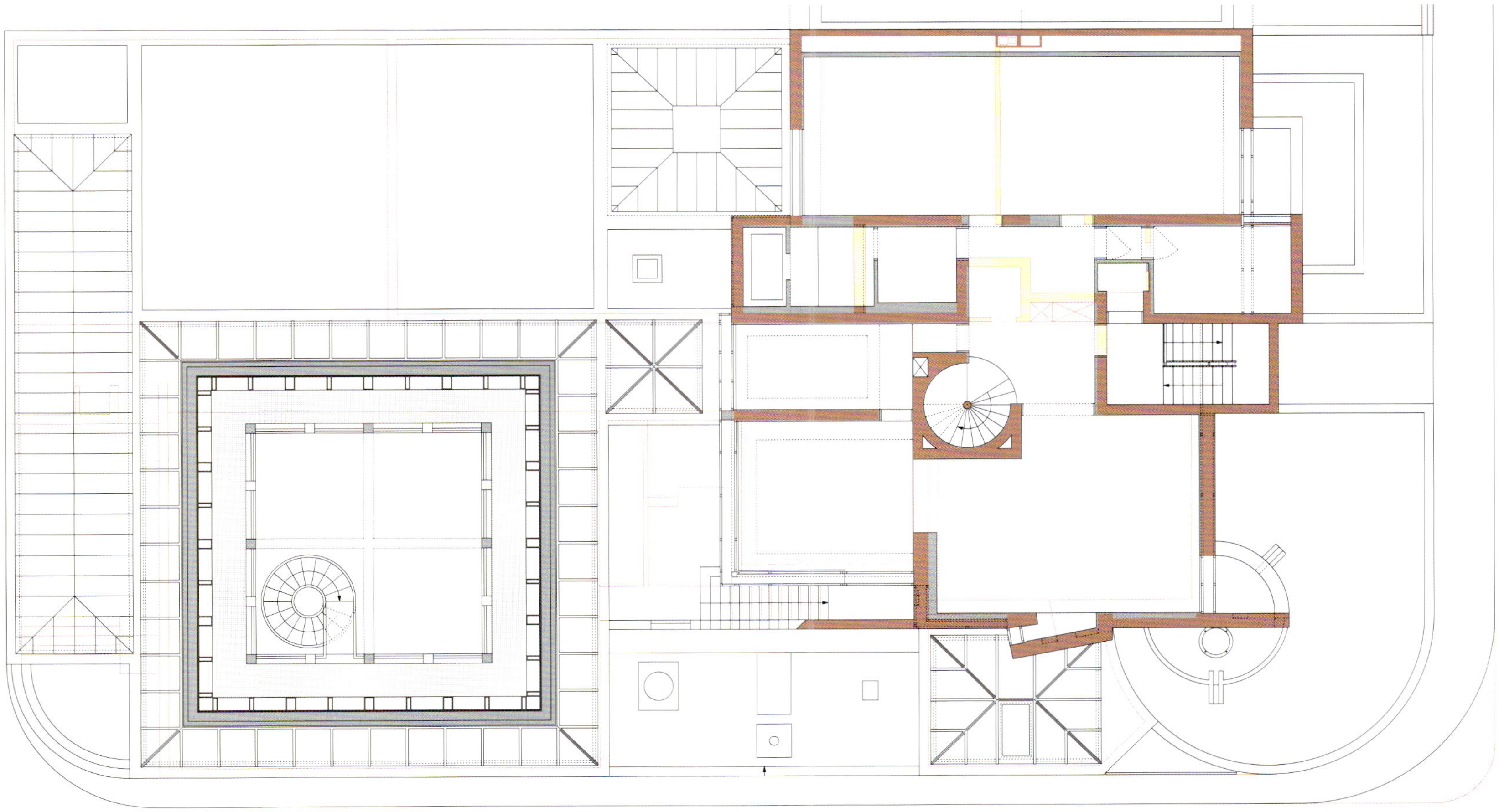

23. Gesamtansicht von Westen, 1991. (Photo: Dieter Leistner.)
24. Dachterrasse im Dachgeschoß, 1991. (Photo: Bernd Grimm.)
25. Blick von oben auf die Bibliothek und dem ihr vorgelagerten Innenhof, 1991. (Photo: Dieter Leistner.)

23. General view form the west, 1991. (Photo: Dieter Leistner.)
24. Roof terrace on the attic floor, 1991. (Photo: Bernd Grimm.)
25. View of the library and the adjacent courtyard from above, 1991. (Photo: Dieter Leistner.)

26. Innenhof vor der Bibliothek mit toskanischen Säulen, 1991. (Photo: Dieter Leistner.)
27. Innenhof vor der Bibliothek mit *Square* von Bruce Naumann und *Basalt Circle* von Richard Long, 2000. (Photo: Dieter Leistner.)

26. Courtyard in front of the library with Tuscan columns, 1991. (Photo: Dieter Leistner.)
27. Courtyard in front of the library with *Square* by Bruce Naumann and *Basalt Circle* by Richard Long, 2000. (Photo: Dieter Leistner.)

28. Zentraler Durchgang im Erdgeschoß in Richtung Hauseingang, 1996. (Photo: Stefan Müller.)
29. Zeichenraum in der ehemaligen Einliegerwohnung im Erdgeschoß, 1996. (Photo: Stefan Müller.)

28. Central passage on the ground floor viewing toward the house entrance, 1996. (Photo: Stefan Müller.)
29. Drawing room in the former granny-flat on the ground floor, 1996. (Photo: Stefan Müller.)

30. Wohnraum mit Blick in den Speiseraum im Obergeschoß, 1991. (Photo: Dieter Leistner.)
31. Blick vom Vorraum mit der zentralen Wendeltreppe in den Wohnraum im Obergeschoß, 1991. (Photo: Dieter Leistner.)

30. Living room with view into the dining room on the upper floor, 1991. (Photo: Dieter Leistner.)
31. View from the anteroom with the central spiral stair into the living room on the upper floor, 1991. (Photo: Dieter Leistner.)

32. Blick vom Vorraum in den Besprechungsraum in der ehemaligen Einliegerwohnung im Obergeschoß, 2007. (Photo: Stefan Müller.)
33. Der Besprechungsraum in der ehemaligen Einliegerwohnung im Obergeschoß, 2007. (Photo: Stefan Müller.)

32. View from the anteroom into the conference room in the former granny-flat on the upper floor, 2007. (Photo: Stefan Müller.)
33. The conference room in the former granny-flat on the upper floor, 2007. (Photo: Stefan Müller.)

34. Ausstellung in der ehemaligen Einliegerwohnung im Erdgeschoß, 2011. (Photo: Bernd Grimm.)
35. Der jetzt als Ausstellungsraum genutzte ehemalige Wohnraum im Obergeschoß, 2007. (Photo: Stefan Müller.)

S. 60, 61
36, 37. Die Bibliothek, 1990. Auf der Galerie acht der zwölf aufgesockelten Gipsabgüsse eines antiken Apollokopfes mit dem Titel *The Twelve Who Ruled* von Ian Hamilton Finlay. (Photos: Stefan Müller.)

34. Exhibition in the former granny-flat on the ground floor, 2011. (Photo: Bernd Grimm.)
35. The former living room on the upper floor now used as an exhibition room, 2007. (Photo: Stefan Müller.)

pp. 60, 61
36, 37. The library, 1990. On the gallery eight of the twelve plaster casts, raised on plinths, of an ancient head of Apollo, titled *The Twelve Who Ruled* by Ian Hamilton Finlay. (Photos: Stefan Müller.)

38. Detailansicht der Empore in der Bibliothek, 1990. (Photo: Stefan Müller.)
39. Blick auf die Stele mit einem Gipsabguß der Büste Karl Friedrich Schinkels von Christian Friedrich Tieck von 1819 im Umgang der Bibliothek. 1990. (Photos: Stefan Müller.)

38. Detailed view of the gallery in the library. (Photo: Stefan Müller.)
39. View of the stele with a plaster cast of the bust of Karl Friedrich Schinkel by Christian Friedrich Tieck from 1819 in the ambulatory of the library, 1990. (Photo: Stefan Müller.)

Haus und Bibliothek Ungers
Ungers house and library
Belvederestraße 60
50933 Köln-Müngersdorf

Bauzeit / Construction period
Haus / house: 1958/59
Bibliothek / library: 1989/90

Bauherrin / Client
Liselotte Ungers

Architekt
Oswald Mathias Ungers
Mitarbeiter / Collaborators: Ch. Türke, R. Gerber (Haus / house); M. Croce, B. Grimm (Bibliothek / library)